PRAISE FOR *THE ART OF MINGLING*

"Anyone who reads [*The Art of Mingling*] will end up being the belle of the ball. . . . I love it. I love it. I love it."

—Marabelle Young Stewart

"Having all my life dreaded social mingling with an ever-increasing unease, I will now carry *The Art of Mingling* with me wherever I go, knowing I will no longer be at a loss for words."

—J. P. Donleavy

"Jeanne Martinet, the acid-tongued queen of the New York party scene, has come to the rescue of wallflowers everywhere with *The Art of Mingling*."

—*Daily Mirror* (U.K.)

"If your idea of absolute terror is a room full of strangers at a party . . . then you'd benefit from *The Art of Mingling*."

—*Single Life* magazine

"*The Art of Mingling* takes the intimidation out of party scenes, whether they are business-related or social."

—*Publishers Weekly*

Also by Jeanne Martinet

The Faux Pas Survival Guide
Getting Beyond "Hello"
Come-Ons, Comebacks, and Kiss-Offs
Artful Dodging
Truer Than True Romance

The ART of

proven techniques for mastering any room

 St. Martin's Griffin

New York

Mingling

JEANNE martinet

www.stmartins.com

Book design by Susan Walsh

Library of Congress Cataloging-in-Publication Data

Martinet, Jeanne,
    The art of mingling : proven techniques for mastering any room / Jeanne Martinet.
        p. cm.
    Includes index.
    ISBN-13: 978-0-312-35431-2
    ISBN-10: 0-312-35431-2
    1. Conversation.   2. Interpersonal communication.   3. Etiquette.   I. Title.
BJ2121.M37   2006
158.2'7—dc22   2006047466

10   9   8   7   6   5   4   3   2

To my dear friend Jason—
still the nicest minglephobe I know

Contents

Preface to the New Edition   xiii

Introduction   xv

1   Overcoming Minglephobia   1

HOW TO FAKE IT TILL YOU MAKE IT   1

FOUR SURVIVAL FANTASIES FOR THE TRULY TERRIFIED   2
The Naked Room ○ *The Invisible Man* ○ *The Buddy System*
○ *Pros and Icons*

CHOOSING YOUR FIRST CLIQUE   7
Practice Your Mingle on the Socially Challenged ○ *Judging a
Book by Its Cover* ○ *Body Language Check*
○ *The Safety of Numbers*

2   Open Sesame: Making a Successful Entrance   13

RESTRAINING ORDERS   13
To Shake or Not to Shake ○ *A Word About Smiling*
○ *The Philosophy of Fibbing: Why Lying Is Essential*

THE FOUR BASIC ENTRANCE MANEUVERS   17
The Honest Approach ○ *The Fade-in* ○ *The Flattery Entrée*
○ *The Sophistication Test*

OPENING LINES FOR EVERY MOOD   24
Level One: The Risk-free Line ○ *Level Two: The Playful Line*
○ *Level Three: The Daring Line*

3 Now What? Tools and Rules for
Continuing the Conversation   29

RECOVERING FROM A FLUBBED OPENING   30

CAREER TALK: YES OR NO?   32

AN ABCEDARY FOR THOSE AT A LOSS FOR WORDS   36

TRIED-AND-TRUE TRICKS OF THE TRADE   43
Name-Tag Tips ○ *The Interview* ○ *Playing a Game* ○ *Party
Favors: The Helpless Hannah Ploy* ○ *Room with a View*
○ *Using Clichés* ○ *About Eye Contact* ○ *The Dot-Dot-Dot Plot*
○ *The Echo Chamber* ○ *The Funny Thing About Humor*
○ *How to Handle the Joker in Every Deck*

4 The Great Escape: Bailing Out and Moving On   61

WHEN TO MOVE   63
Boredom and Other Discomforts ○ *Saving Face* ○ *The Case
of the Vanishing Group* ○ *Time's Up!*

THE ETIQUETTE OF ESCAPE   65
Knowing Where You're Headed ○ *The Five Laws of Survival*

THE GETAWAY: TWELVE EXIT MANEUVERS   67
The Honest Approach in Reverse ○ *The Fade-out*
○ *The Changing of the Guard* ○ *The Smooth Escape*
○ *Shake and Break* ○ *The Human Sacrifice* ○ *The Personal
Manager* ○ *Escape by Mutual Consent* ○ *The Buffet Bye-Bye
and Other Handy Excuses* ○ *Celling Out* ○ *The Counterfeit
Search* ○ *The Preemptive Strike: Dodgeball*

EMERGENCY ESCAPE HATCHES   79

5 Fancy Footwork: Advanced Mingling
Techniques   81

MINGLING STYLES FOR THE WELL SCHOOLED   81
The Quick-Change Artist ○ *The Pole-Vaulter* ○ *The Playful
Plagiarist* ○ *Trivial Pursuits* ○ *The Art of Piggybacking*
○ *The Butterfly Flit*

GIMMICKS FOR THE CONFIDENT MINGLER   91
A Case of Mistaken Identity ○ *Fumbling In* ○ *The Interruption
Eruption* ○ *The Quotation Device* ○ *Making the Most
of Toasts*

SOPHISTICATED BODY BUSINESS   99
The Mysterious Mingle ○ *The Touchy-Feely Mingle*
○ *The Beauty of Bowing*

CONVERSATION PIECES: USING PROPS   104
Jewelry and Accessories ○ *Gadgets and Other Paraphernalia*
○ *The Hors D'oeuvre Maneuver* ○ *Working the Bar
or Food Area*

PLAYING DOUBLES: TEAM MINGLING   110
Preparty Strategy Sessions ○ *Conversational Procurement*
○ *Intraparty Play Dates* ○ *Shepherding* ○ *Reconnaissance
and Rescue* ○ *The Mating Call*

6 Under Fire: Handling Unusual Situations   117
LIE OR DIE   117
DEALING WITH FAUX PAS   118
When You're Dressed Wrong ○ *Introductions: A Recurring
Nightmare* ○ *Storytelling as a Healing Technique* ○ *All-Purpose
Faux Pas Recovery Lines* ○ *The Faux Pas Moi: The Art
of Denial* ○ *The Faux Pas-cifist*

NEGOTIATING TOUGH ROOMS   133

The Sardine Can ○ *The Thin Room* ○ *Mingling with Drunks*
○ *Mingling with the Truly Arrogant*

THE SIT-DOWN MINGLE   141

QUICK FIXES FOR DIRE CIRCUMSTANCES   143
How to React to Hand Kissing and Other Unwelcome
Physicalities ○ *Handling Insults* ○ *All-Purpose Lines for*
Treating Panic ○ *Cutting Your Losses (or, When to Just*
Give Up and Go Home)

7 Mingling in the Twenty-first Century   149

NAVIGATING CURRENT EVENTS   151
The Zeitgeist Heist ○ *Pleading Guilty* ○ *Proving Your Mettle*
○ *Warning: High-Voltage Area! Talking Politics*

AHOY POLLOI: MINGLING IN PUBLIC PLACES   159
Mingling Outdoors or in a Crowd ○ *Lines in Line*
○ *Elevator Mingling*

MINGLING FOR LOVE   167
Venue Tips ○ *Romance Copilots* ○ *Love Lines*

HOSTING: HOW TO PLEASE YOUR GUESTS EVERY TIME   173
Host Phobia ○ *The Party Coach* ○ *The Feng Shui of Hosting*

8 From Insecurity to Enlightenment:
The Tao of Mingling   177

WU WEI: PREMINGLE MEDITATION   178

THE YIN/YANG OF CIRCULATING   179

THE ART OF YIELDING: USING THE PRINCIPLES OF TAI CHI   180

HOW TO FEEL HAPPY WHEN YOU ARE LEFT ALONE   182

Index   185

Preface to the New Edition

Like all my best ideas, *The Art of Mingling* was born on a cocktail napkin. In the wee hours of the morning after a wedding in Dayton, Ohio, I was hanging out with college friends, performing a group postmortem on the reception. Suddenly one of my friends said to me rather accusingly, "Hey, Jeanne, how did you manage to meet everyone in the entire town? The rest of us only talked to people we already knew." More to entertain than to instruct, I proceeded to jot down on a napkin some of my mingling techniques (which until that point in time I never realized I had names for). To my amazement, my audience was not merely entertained but actually hungry for this information. That's when I realized that I was much more in touch with the methods of mingling than other people were and that people were eager to learn these methods.

Still, when the *The Art of Mingling* was first published in 1992 I was not completely aware of the amount of mingling-related fear that existed. In identifying this pervasive social phobia and in offering my own personal and practical system for socializing at parties it seems I had struck a societal nerve. Even the most surprising kinds of people—TV talk show hosts, radio personalities, top executives—have revealed to me that not only are they terrified of making small talk with strangers, but also my approach struck a chord with them. People seem to really want to improve their abilities in this area. They wanted to become better, more confident minglers.

Unfortunately, fourteen years and as many printings later, people are more minglephobic than ever. We live in a world of e-mail, Web sites, and cell phones; and although we may have better diets, faster trains, and more cable channels, we are less adept at standing in a room with real-live people and not shriveling up in a heap of nervous twitches and stammers. Our mingling muscles, if we had any, have atrophied.

In this new edition I have updated many of the references and real-life scenarios, as well as the techniques themselves. In addition, for the last ten years I have been collecting new "field-tested" mingling tips and lines, which I have added throughout to offer the reader more mingling options. I have added two much-needed new chapters: "Mingling in the Twenty-first Century" and "The Tao of Mingling."

It has become one of my missions in life to encourage everyone to get out there and talk to one another. As with any other kind of exploration, it's always safer if you stay home, but remember: Nothing can be gained if you don't venture out into the unknown, and fewer things in life are more delicious than an engaging, spontaneous conversation with someone new.

Introduction

You are at a cocktail party. The decor is delightful; the guests are glamorous; the food is fabulous—nothing could be more wonderful, right?

Wrong. It's a nightmare. You want desperately to disappear. Everywhere around you are people who seem to know each other. They are talking and laughing, having a great time, while you are standing against the wall, wishing with all your heart that you were somewhere else—anywhere else—but here. Two firm convictions keep you from dying on the spot: (1) There's no question about it. You are going to take the life of the (ex-) friend who somehow convinced you that you needed to expand your horizons by coming to this party and (2) if this night ever ends, you will *never ever* leave the safety of your home again.

An exaggeration? Maybe. But I know plenty of people, of all ages and from all walks of life, who are perfectly comfortable with the one-on-one or the small-group social interaction but confess to a secret terror of medium-to-large parties of any kind. The very *idea* of having to talk to a lot of people they don't know makes them go dry in the mouth and shaky in the knees. They'll do *anything* to avoid mingling situations. Many opt out, telling themselves they are skipping the party because they have too much to do at the office or they are too tired to go—even that they have nothing to wear! This is a shame bordering on a tragedy, because larger affairs—whether they be business or "social" functions—are potentially much more exciting and energizing than small get-togethers. They are fertile arenas for meeting new people, and yet, simply because of their apprehension, people often waste good opportunities either by not going to a party or by going with a colleague or companion and sticking to him like glue. Anything, they think, is better than to risk being left standing all alone, looking pathetic and ridiculous. And even *that* is preferable to suffering the incomparable agony of being face-to-face with a stranger and not knowing what to say.

People who feel this way (and there are more of them out there than you can imagine) have a widespread disease known as *minglephobia*. Is there a cure? Yes. Because contrary to what you might think, "making conversation," "being a social butterfly," or "working the room" is a learned art—a simple one—which *anyone* can master.

It's true that social skills *seem* to come more easily to some than others, and there are a lucky few who are actually born mingling geniuses (in fact, I once saw a three-year-old boy work a room so well it was scary). But even the pathetically shy, the tongue-tied, and the foot-in-mouth types can learn simple techniques, tricks, lines, and maneuvers that can mean the difference between fun and misery, between a night of total humiliation and one of social ecstasy.

Of course, there are those few misguided souls who think mingling is simply a waste of time; that it is nothing but an endless stream of meaningless conversations with people you will never see again. And yes, I admit I've had my share of inane discussions about weather or traffic. But I've also had countless ten-minute conversations about supposedly trivial subjects like wallpaper that were memorable and fun, after which I've usually gone home feeling happy and more connected to the world. You must never forget that simply being in a room full of people who are communicating with each other is exhilarating! Just look up "mingle" in the dictionary: "to be or become mixed or united or to become closely associated; join or take part with others." Sounds stimulating, even sexy, doesn't it? It is. I know from experience.

I'll tell you a secret. Although I have always adored parties—anywhere, anytime—mingling didn't come naturally to me at all. When I was about thirteen, I made up my mind that I would become a mingling virtuoso. I proceeded to teach myself the art over the course of years, by trial and error. I have collected tips and adapted techniques from countless friends and acquaintances, as well as from books (mostly old ones, from previous eras when every well-brought-up person was highly proficient in the art of conversation). All the methods I use have been tested and honed for best results, and now I have a system that never fails. It's easy, and you can learn it, too.

Each of the following techniques and lines is applicable to just about any type of large gathering. However, there's one fundamental principle to remember as you begin to study this time-honored art: *Your purpose in any mingling situation is to have fun.* This is an absolutely vital, hard-and-fast rule; your success as a mingler depends on your following this basic premise. Whether you are at a business affair or a neighbor's party, whether you are mingling for love or for career advancement (incidentally, I think we've all had enough of the word "networking"; I myself refuse to use it except in the context of fishing!), your primary goal *must* be your own enjoyment. You may see a given mingling situation as a means to climbing the proverbial corporate ladder or hooking up with a hottie, but unless you truly enjoy meeting and talking with people, your success will be limited. The truth is that mingling is its own reward.

So, take a deep breath, and *let's mingle!*

1 Overcoming Minglephobia

HOW TO FAKE IT TILL YOU MAKE IT

OK. There you are, standing alone, frozen against the wall in a room full of people. You've just arrived, and you've already done the two things that made you look busy: taken off your coat and said hello to your host or hostess, who has long since dashed off to greet another guest or check on the ice supply. What now?

Number one (and numbers two and three): Don't panic. You are not the only person feeling this way. Many people descend into a state of existential angst when faced with tough mingling situations. Some people deal with their fears by withdrawing into a corner; others become nervous or clumsy. Some giggle; some play with their hair or fiddle with their clothing. In fact, minglephobia can cause people to drink too much, eat too much, smoke too much, or—and this can really be dangerous—even dance too much! So it's important not to give in to your fears, especially in those first few crucial moments. Just try to relax and say to yourself, *I'm going to fake it till I make it.*

Believe it or not, this simple affirmation is an effective, almost magical, way to transform party terror into a positive outlook. Remember when you were little and you used to tell ghost stories to scare yourself and by the end of the night you really did believe in ghosts? It was amazingly easy to fool yourself when you were a child, and it's just as easy to fool yourself as an adult. Just pretend to be happy to be wherever you are; make believe you are confident; simulate self-assurance—even for ten minutes—and an amazing thing will start to happen: You'll actually begin to feel that way, partially because of the response you receive from other people.

Let's face it. Very few people want to talk to someone who is showing outward signs of fear or depression. (Unless it's a Goth or fetish party. But that's a whole other book.) So even though you will probably have at least some apprehension when approaching people you know little or not at all, you must practice putting it aside. Just as if you had to walk out on a stage. Deep breath. Curtain up. Before you know it, you'll discover you're no longer faking it, that your fears have disappeared and you are actually having a good time!

Fake It Till You Make It is an attitude aid rather than a specific technique, but it's important to remember it as you begin to mingle, because it is the basis of all the opening gambits and entry lines. Your mind-set as you enter the fray is extremely important. For the first few minutes of a difficult mingling experience, what you *project* is more important than what you may be feeling.

FOUR SURVIVAL FANTASIES FOR THE TRULY TERRIFIED

Sometimes the Fake It Till You Make It mantra isn't enough when you are faced with a room full of Serious Terror Inducers. Serious Terror Inducers are usually defined as people with whom you feel you have nothing in common. The scariest groups for me are investment bankers, people at East Hampton art gallery openings, or the women's bridge club in Provo, Utah. But whether your own worst mingling nightmare is a singles' soiree or your own block association picnic, and whether you are attending a high-pressure business affair or a holiday cocktail party, the following survival fantasies can be life-savers. They are for those times when you can hardly breathe, when you can't remember your name or the name of the person who invited you, when you suddenly have no idea why you were invited and suspect that someone's secretary must have made a horrible mistake in adding you to the guest list.

The need for this kind of psychological armor varies greatly, of course, with each individual and situation. Extraordinarily shy people and people who haven't been out of the house for two months may use the survival fantasies regularly. Some people (like me) find the fantasies to be so much fun that they use them all the time for the pure kick they get out of them. But in any case, they can provide you with an instant shot of social confidence, enough to allow you to approach a group of intimidating strangers. All you need to make them work is a little imagination.

The Naked Room

Suppose you have just arrived at a large party. As you enter the room, you realize that (1) you don't know a soul there; (2) everyone is talking animatedly; and (3) the second you walked in, you lost every ounce of self-assurance you ever had.

Try this: Just for a moment, imagine that everyone in the room—except for you—is wearing nothing but their underclothes (preferably raggedy ones) and shoes. There are variations, naturally, according to what you think makes people look the most ridiculous and powerless; some people prefer to visualize them in only socks, ties, and jewelry, or in their pajamas, or even completely naked. You can try to imagine them all as four-year-olds. But whatever version works for you, the Naked Room fantasy can be an easy way to turn the tables when you're feeling vulnerable or exposed and is an excellent place to start to build your party confidence. Old acquaintances will wonder what the devil has put that secret smile on your face, and strangers will be intrigued by your cocky demeanor.

The Invisible Man

This fantasy is based on a very simple truth, something my mother used to tell me all the time. *Nobody is looking at you. Everyone is too busy worrying about themselves.* While this may not be 100 percent true, it is mostly true. The Invisible Man fantasy merely capitalizes on this basic fact, taking it one step further. Ready? You're just *not there*. You don't exist. Do you think someone's looking at you, wondering snidely why no one is talking to you? You're wrong; everyone's looking right through you *because they can't see you*. They're looking at the food table, at the wall, at another guest. Remember in the 1933 film *The Invisible Man* when Claude Rains took off his bandages and was totally transparent? What power he had! How he laughed! Now, invisible as you are, you are free to unself-consciously walk around the room, looking at everyone, looking at the furniture, the paintings—the whole scene—with total relaxation. This gives you time to catch your breath, psychologically, until you feel ready to become visible again and enter the conversational clique of your choice. (*Warning:* The true introvert may want to be careful with this one; you don't want to stay invisible for too long. I suggest timing yourself for the first couple of tries. *Reappearance is an absolute must.*)

The Buddy System

Remember in elementary school when you went on field trips and your teacher used to make you line up with a partner so that no one would get lost? In my school, they called this the Buddy System. Well, here you are now, feeling virtually "lost" in this room full of intimidating strangers. How can you possibly get up the nerve to speak to anyone?

Easy. You and your best buddy will go together. Tell yourself that just behind you, over your right shoulder, your very best friend in the whole world is moving with you through the room, listening to everything you say. Voilà: instant calm. After all, your friend loves you, right? Understands you? And probably will have a lot of the same opinions of the people you meet as you do. When you talk, you will be able to imagine this friend smiling at everything you say, offering encouragement and approval. If by chance you are snubbed by some ignorant dolt, you'll hear your friend whisper in your ear, *What a jerk!*

Of course, you mustn't get carried away and actually *speak* to your imaginary friend (at least not so anyone can notice).

Pros and Icons

This technique is kind of the Invisible Man fantasy in reverse. It may seem drastic to some people, but I find it so effective, as well as so much fun, that I highly recommend it, especially for the more adventuresome. Don't forget, these fantasy techniques are specifically designed for *initial* courage; to get you to take that first step, to transform you from a wallflower with an inferiority complex into a participating, mingling member of the party. So try this: *Be someone else,* just for a little while. This might seem a bit radical, especially since other people have probably been telling you for decades to "be yourself," but if you're standing there at the party terrified, halfway wishing you were somebody else anyway, then why not just do it? The person that you are is giving you a lot of trouble right now and is obviously not the least bit happy about where he is. So pick a favorite celebrity, someone whose poise, posture, or personality you particularly admire, and then . . . slip into him or her. When done right, this technique works much more quickly than the other survival fantasies, because of the mingling power most people attribute to stars—power that instantly becomes accessible to you.

I used to become Bette Davis, especially when faced with really tough rooms or if I was just feeling insecure for some reason. I would visualize her in one of her movie roles, usually as Margot Channing in *All About Eve*, and pretty soon I would sense my eyebrows going up slightly and my body relaxing as I surveyed the social battlefield with a truly languid amusement. As Bette Davis (or, more specifically, Davis in the role of Margot) I would not just be *ready* to mingle; I'd be positively *hungry* for it. No one, by the way, ever looked over at me and said, "Look at that weird woman pretending to be Bette Davis!" because no one, of course, ever noticed the difference. They merely saw a confident—perhaps even interesting—woman. Likewise, no one will be able to tell what you are doing when you use this technique. After all, that's why these are called fantasies—they're *secret*. Also, you don't *have* to use a celebrity. You can, if you want, pretend to be someone you know in real life, someone who is never ill at ease (or, more likely, who never *seems* to be ill at ease—she probably feels the same as you do inside, of course). The only guideline is that you must choose someone you know pretty well; the better you know this person, the easier it is to assume his or her persona.

Some favorite Pros and Icons for women: Ingrid Bergman, Campbell Brown, Katie Couric, Bette Davis, Kirsten Dunst, Goldie Hawn, Katharine Hepburn, Scarlett Johansson, Grace Kelly, Vivien Leigh (as Scarlett, of course), Reese Witherspoon, Jennifer Lopez, Madonna, Marilyn Monroe, Jackie Onassis, Sarah Jessica Parker, Julia Roberts, Diane Sawyer, Gertrude Stein, Venus Williams, Oprah Winfrey, and Catherine Zeta-Jones. Men can use Antonio Banderas, Humphrey Bogart, Tom Brady, Pierce Brosnan, George Clooney,

Johnny Depp, Leonardo DiCaprio, Harrison Ford, Jamie Foxx, Bill
Gates, Cary Grant, LeBron James, Derek Jeter, Larry King, David
Niven, Jack Nicholson, Brad Pitt, Jerry Seinfeld, Jon Stewart, Den-
zel Washington, or even Prince William. *Please note:* It's best not to
use people who are charismatic but may actually be frightening
(such as the Rock, Michael Jackson, Christopher Walken, or Janice
Dickinson).

o   O   o

Each of these survival fantasies will take some practice, particularly
if you've never tried anything like this before. But believe me, they
will help, especially if you are a person who tends to freeze, to one
degree or another, at the very beginning of a difficult mingling experience. You may also develop your own personalized survival
fantasy—one that works better for you than any of the ones I have
outlined—and that's fine, of course.

And now, bolstered by the survival fantasy of your choice, you are
ready to enter the ring, to approach a person or persons—to get to the
actual "meat" of mingling.

CHOOSING YOUR FIRST CLIQUE

As in any game or art, deciding where to begin is very important.
Every party, every large gathering, has its bright lights, its superstar
mingle circles, its personality power points. Should you forge ahead
and go right for the loudest, laughingest, most powerful enclave of
people in the room?

Absolutely not! Not unless you consider yourself on the interme-
diate to advanced level in the art of mingling. After all, you've just
gone through at least one survival fantasy to get you this far, and you

don't want to blow it now by getting shot down by the coolest guest at the party. First you need to get in some relatively safe practice.

Practice Your Mingle on the Socially Challenged

That's right. Scope out the wimpiest, limpest, nerdiest soul in the whole room. This will vary from party to party; it's all relative. Usually it's a quiet person, but not always. (Sometimes it's someone who is laughing way too loud.) He may be inappropriately dressed or at least not completely well put-together. Lots of times you can identify this party misfit by his lost, timid expression or shuffling stance or by the way he appears fascinated by one of the wall fixtures. At any rate, you must think of this first person or cluster of people (perhaps even several clusters, depending on how much practice you need) as your sketch pad, your scratch paper, your dress rehearsal. The PSAT of your mingling experience.

Keep in mind as you approach this person or group that your main purpose here is to learn how certain kinds of conversation work on people, how they feel to you. Did a certain line come naturally to you, or did it sound rehearsed? Was it perhaps executed with the wrong inflection? Because you are interacting with the party's lowest common denominator, you can try out mingling techniques you'd ordinarily never dare to try. It's like practicing your swimming in the shallow end of the pool before venturing into the deep end. Of course, you must always remember, when you are "practicing your mingle" with the socially challenged, that the reaction you get is not necessarily the reaction you can expect from one of the party's bright wits. Nevertheless, the opportunity to practice is invaluable for the minglephobe and should be taken advantage of whenever possible.

There is, as you might have guessed, an added benefit to this technique: Some of the most fascinating people in the world happen to be severely socially challenged. While getting in some stress-free practice with your misfit, you may accidentally have the conversation of a lifetime.

Judging a Book by Its Cover

If you can't find any socially challenged people to practice on, there is another very effective way to choose a safe and easy mingling target. I learned this method while watching my father, a musician, at a rather stuffy party of mostly lawyers and bankers. He stood there, scoping out the party, not talking to anyone, for about fifteen minutes.

Typical Dad, I thought, *totally antisocial.* Suddenly he made a bee-line for a man standing in the corner. Before long, the two of them were engrossed in conversation, laughing away. Curious, I joined them. ("Hey, Dad" is, by the way, always a good entrance line!) The "subject" my father had singled out was a journalist and turned out to be rather a kindred spirit to my father. I noted that they talked on and off for the entire evening.

Later I asked my father how he had chosen this man to talk to, out of all the people at the party. "Easy," he replied. "He was the only man there without a suit and tie on." My father, who never wears a suit and tie if he can help it, had selected his first mingling subject on the basis of similar taste in clothes, on the assumption that the man's attire was an indication of a creative personality. And Dad was right!

Fact one: You can often tell a lot about a person by appearance. Fact two: It is almost always easier to converse with someone who is similar to you than to someone who is dissimilar (though it might not be as interesting). Therefore, if you choose a person who is dressed as you are or even as you would *like* to be dressed, your chances of a comfortable—mayhe even fun   exchange are increased. Because you are at the very beginning of your mingling and you're nervous, it's vital that your first couple of encounters go well, or you may give up and go home before you've even begun to mingle.

Body Language Check

If you were to enter a room where everyone was sitting, the first thing you would do is look for an empty chair. In most mingling situations, you're going to be entering a room where everyone is standing (more or less), but you still need to find an open spot. Examining body language will help you to find a person or group of people who will be receptive to talking to you.

I don't mean that you should stand around for a long time analyzing your surroundings until you suddenly realize there is no food left and everyone has gone home. With a cursory scan you can fairly quickly ascertain which people are "open" and which are "closed." If, on the one hand, you see three people in a tight circle who are laughing hysterically or talking intently with their arms around each other, this is a closed group and will be hard to enter. If, on the other hand, you see two people standing loosely together, looking around the room with pleasant (but hopefully not vapid) expressions on their faces, this is an open situation. Most enclaves will fall somewhere in between these two extremes, of course. Take a quick inventory: Is there space between people's bodies? Is someone in the group looking out at the party population in general? Are they leaning in toward each other, as if they don't want anyone to overhear them? Trying to join two people who are talking earnestly to each other is riskiest; if their eyes never leave each other's faces you might take it as a Do Not Disturb sign.

The Safety of Numbers

When making that all-important decision of whom to approach first, keep in mind one of the simplest, oldest maxims in the history of human interaction: *There is safety in numbers.* Whether you are making a gentle approach or a boisterously dramatic entrance, your chances of avoiding total disgrace are statistically better with a larger group of people. Either everyone will notice you as soon as you enter the circle and, because there are so many people, some of them (at least one, anyhow) are bound to be polite, or no one will notice you joining the group, giving you ample time to listen, digest the different personalities, and choose an appropriate opening line—or escape from the clique totally unscathed, a virtual mingling virgin.

In general, the larger the group, the larger your range of options. Perhaps most important, in a large group you will almost definitely not die the horrible death of awkward silence, something that *can* happen to you when you are involved with a cluster of two or even three people.

Of course, the best defense against awkward silences is a great opening.

Open Sesame: Making a Successful Entrance

RESTRAINING ORDERS

Now you've selected a mingling target group and you're ready to make your entrance. Before we get to the specific openings, there are still a few things to consider.

To Shake or Not to Shake

This is not about how to stop trembling in fear. This is about that age-old custom of handclasping, traditionally thought to be purely a matter of etiquette and—in most business settings—as natural as breathing.

The fact is that I have found handshaking to be a precarious practice in many mingling situations. Often it interrupts any conversation that is already flowing among the circle of people you are entering, not to mention that many people are holding drinks, food, or other items in their hands. It also can punctuate, more loudly than you may want, the fact that you have officially joined the group. So, although most of us are trained by our parents that it is polite to shake hands with people when first meeting them, my own rule for entering a group of more than two people *is not to shake* unless introduced to someone by a third person. There are exceptions to this directive; some approaches or opening lines necessitate a handshake, and, of course, sometimes someone else initiates a handshake.

Men: This is going to be hard for you. For some reason, men love to shake hands, anytime, anywhere. Sew your hands to your pockets if you have to, but *don't stick out that hand unless someone else sticks his or hers out first.*

A Word About Smiling

Everyone has his own personal "smile style," but there are some guidelines to follow regarding smiling at the particular time you are entering a conversational clique. Unless your approach involves the technique of abrupt interruption (see p. 94), I recommend that you either do not smile or that you use a closed-mouthed smile. A toothy smile can seem too cheery, and there is something decidedly off-putting, even odd, about a total stranger approaching you with an enormous grin on her face. It's distracting, to say the least, and makes the recipient wonder if he's being laughed at. On the other hand, a closed-mouthed or toothless smile is mysterious, sophisticated, and subtle. Remember, you don't want to scare off the group you're joining! As usual, there are exceptions to this rule, but you'd probably know if you were one of them. For example, I know someone whose smile is so powerful, whose teeth are so white, that it almost hurts your eyes. His smile radiates personality anywhere he goes, and people actually gather around him just to warm themselves by his pearly whites. He floats in and out of groups without following the closed-smile rule, without knowing the first thing about mingling, in fact. Obviously, if you have a nuclear smile like this, you should use it, teeth and all, as much as you want to (maybe *more* than you want to!).

In any case, you shouldn't worry too much about your smile, as too much worrying can cause weird things to happen to your mouth.

Most people don't realize when they are smiling and how, and that's perfectly OK. But if you would like to remember the rule about smiling, here's a little rhyme to memorize:

> *When going in,*
> *No toothful grin.*
> *Use, for a while,*
> *The closed-mouthed smile.*
> *After a clever remark,*
> *The lips may part.*

The Philosophy of Fibbing: Why Lying Is Essential

Before we go any further it is important that I broach a touchy subject. Here it is: *You can't be a good mingler unless you are willing to lie.*

I am sometimes accused of being a sneaky, insincere sort of person, merely because many of my social strategies and solutions happen to be based on fibbing. These idealists believe that we would all be better off if everyone just told the truth all the time. I watched one of these "Honest Abes" in action at a barbecue in upstate New York one weekend. He was standing with me and a friend of mine when a woman approached, calling the Honest Abe by name. As the woman leaned forward for a greeting kiss, Abe put out his hand and said crisply, "I'd rather not kiss. Let's just shake hands."

The newcomer was visibly embarrassed. I was embarrassed *for* her. My friend was also embarrassed. We all stood there awkwardly while the proposed handshaking took place. The woman chatted with us for a minute but left as soon as she could. When she was gone I asked Abe just what the heck was going on between him and the would-be kisser. Abe told me that they were acquaintances, that there was nothing in particular between them. He went on to explain that he had been merely practicing his new policy of total honesty. Apparently Abe didn't care for greeting kisses and he was quite proud of his newfound ability to clearly communicate his needs and feelings.

I had to bite my tongue (and believe me that's not a wise thing to do while you are eating spicy barbecue) to keep from asking Abe what had happened to his manners. Self-realization and personal integrity notwithstanding, how hard would it have been for Abe to have sacrificed his dedication to the truth just enough to add, "I think I may be catching a cold," to his rebuff? Better yet, it would have been a fairly simple matter for him to have physically parried the kiss and just shaken the woman's hand without making any sort of verbal confrontation out of it.

Too many people today pride themselves on being absolutely truthful when the greater truth is that the fabric of society is held together by an intricate weaving of gentle deceptions and subterfuges. Seemingly, decades of self-improvement workshops, 12-step programs, group therapy, and communication seminars have trained people to be more direct in expressing their feelings. But somewhere along the way we lost something very important, and honesty has become a highly overrated commodity.

Don't get me wrong. I *am* in favor of truth-telling when it comes to marriage counseling, court testimony, memoirs, and tax returns. But when you have just approached a stranger at a party, you simply cannot say, "It's not that I really want to talk to you; it's just that you happen to be standing near the cheese."

Being willing and able to tell a white lie is in fact the cornerstone of the art of mingling, the basis from which most of the techniques in this book are taught. A little fibbing enables you to be in control of your social experience—to steer your own course through the party—and at the same time protect your fellow human beings from experiencing any discomfort. Mingling is a dance that is enhanced by the use of tricky steps, and those steps usually involve good-natured old-fashioned prevarication.

I believe that among civilized people a tacit agreement exists: When we are engaging in lighthearted socializing, not every word out of our mouths is the truth. Everyone expects a certain amount of white lying and, in most cases, even appreciates it. We just don't talk about it. (Well, OK, I do!)

THE FOUR BASIC ENTRANCE MANEUVERS

The Honest Approach

Fibbing is fun and effective, but if sincerity is more your style, there's always the Honest Approach.

After you've tried this and experienced the response, you'll be astonished at how few people follow this simple, straightforward course of action. I first tried this opening on a wild impulse when I was feeling overwhelmingly lost at a very stuffy publication party for a prizewinning novelist. I didn't know a soul, and most of the guests were clustered in tight, closed groups of two or three—the hardest kind to enter smoothly. I slipped into a survival fantasy for a few moments, then marched right up to a pleasant-looking man who was totally engrossed in conversation. I stood beside him long enough for him to look over at me (maybe one or two minutes, which can be a lifetime in this situation) and said, "Excuse me, I hope you don't mind my coming up to you out of the blue like this, but I don't know a single soul here. I'm Jeanne Martinet. . . ."

At the time, I thought it was a rather dangerous ploy. Imagine my delight when this fellow, whose name turned out to be Peter, smiled as if I had just handed him a million dollars and told me that he had always wanted to use that approach at a party but had always been too shy, that he thought it was great that I just introduced myself that way. We ended up having a long and enjoyable conversation.

About a week after the party, I actually received a letter from Peter, thanking me for reminding him about an "important interpersonal skill"! This is, I'll admit, an extreme reaction. But I have used the technique many times since then, and it has always worked, to varying degrees (though I never got any more fan mail about it!).

The Honest Approach works because it strikes a familiar chord in almost everyone and because it immediately offers the power to the people you are approaching, creating a nonthreatening situation. You have basically put yourself in their hands. The only trick is, you have to seem sincere. To *seem* sincere, you have to *be* at least partially sincere. Therefore, it is best if you use this approach only when you truly don't know anyone at the event. The other thing to remember about the Honest Approach is that you should use it only once or twice at a specific party. If you use the line on anyone who has already seen you talking intimately to someone at the party, you obviously lose credibility.

Note: This approach *is* one where it's OK, even helpful, to use a handshake. This is because it is *interruptive* in nature and any blatant interruption is already so disruptive that a handshake will act as a communicative salve.

As with many mingling techniques, the Honest Approach will work best if tailored to suit your personality. But whatever words you use, you're bound to have fun finding out that sometimes honesty really *is* the best policy.

The Fade-in

This thief-in-the-night gambit is usually too passive and too slow for my taste, but I know many people who absolutely swear by it. Move as unobtrusively as you can up to the circle of your choice. Listen carefully to everything that's being said as you draw near. The idea is not to be noticed entering the enclave but to become an intrinsic part of it before anyone realizes you're a newcomer. If you pay close attention to the conversation while you are fading in, you'll be able to contribute to it at an appropriate place, as if you had been there all along, taking part in the discussion. If by chance you are discovered before your Fade-in is complete, you will, with any luck, have heard enough to make a pertinent comment and gain immediate acceptance.

The key to the Fade-in is acting as if you absolutely belong there, as if you have been an integral part of this group for hours, as if talking to this specific set of people is what you do for a living. You'll find it is incredibly easy to convince people just by acting as if something is true.

Warning: Be sure to complete your Fade-in. It's crucial that within a fairly short period of time you either complete entry—that is, say something—or move on to another group. The tendency will be, if you're insecure about meeting new people, merely to hang around the periphery, listening and not joining in. This is not mingling! Don't be a party ghost.

The Flattery Entrée

This method may seem self-explanatory, but there's a right way to flatter and a wrong way, especially in mingling situations. While everyone responds to certain kinds of flattery (flattering people about their children or pets is a guaranteed win), there are other kinds that can bomb in a nuclear way. Here's a short quiz to find out how much you already know about flattery:

OPENING LINE	SHOULD YOU USE IT?
1. *"Excuse me, but I couldn't help noticing your beautiful dress [or suit]. I love it! Where did you get it?"*	Yes • No

(continued)

OPENING LINE	SHOULD YOU USE IT?

2. *"Wow! Those are the most
fabulous earrings!"*   Yes   ˒ No

3. *"Excuse me, but from the looks
of you, you must really work
out a lot."*   Yes   ˍ No

4. *"Pardon me, you all seem like
such nice people. Do you mind
if I join you?"*   Yes   ˌ No

5. *"Hi"* (speaking softly). *"Do you
mind if I talk to you guys? I don't
want to sound mean, but you're
the only people here who seem at
all interesting."*   Yes   ˎ No

6. *"Well! Do you mind if I join
this illustrious circle of high-
powered shakers and movers?"*   Yes   ˎ No

7. *"Hello! I heard the laughter from
across the room. Since at least one
of you must be either very funny
or very happy, I decided I'd come
over and see if it might rub off
on me."*   Yes   ˍNo

Now let's see how you did:

1. **It may surprise you, but the correct answer to this one is no.**
   Remember, we are talking about an opening line. The main
   thing about flattery is that it's often better not to use it than to
   risk going overboard. Unless someone is wearing a getup that is

definitely meant to draw comments (and you'd better be sure about this), it's too personal to *open* using this kind of remark with someone you've never met before. To say you love someone's dress is basically the same as saying you like the way she looks, her body, her style, and that's simply too forward for the Flattery Entrée. After you've talked to the person for a while, then you can use this line. Flattery in midmingle is a whole different matter.

2. **Yes.** It's much more appropriate to comment on someone's accessories. It's a tribute to her taste without being too personal. This is also a smart opening because you can follow it up by asking where the person got the earrings and, depending on her answer ("A trip to China," "My boyfriend's mother," "I made them from stuff I found on the street"), you can get a good five or ten minutes' conversation out of it, especially if you're ready to let the response lead you off into exciting new territory! *Warning:* Make sure the person is actually *wearing* earrings before you use this line.

3. **Definitely not.** Not only will this be taken as a blatant come-on, but also it's way too strong, too personal, and too gushy. Gushing is never a good idea unless you already know the person, and even then it's iffy.

4. **This one may seem at first glance to be a possibility, but the answer is no.** First of all, though it seems to smack of the Honest Approach, you can't possibly know these people are nice since you haven't talked to them yet; the comment will seem insincere. Second, it's too wimpy, too "gee-whiz." A wit in the group may shoot you down with, "Well you're wrong, baby. We're all a *terrible* lot—you don't want to associate with us."

5. **No!** Believe it or not, I once thought this might work in some crowds, and I'm always one for experimenting, so one New Year's Eve I tried it out. Boy, was I sorry. What a disaster! The two guys looked at me like I was a leper, and while I was trying to figure out if there was something wrong with my delivery or what, I heard a scandalized voice right behind me, where I thought no one was standing, say, "Of all the nerve!" Horror of horrors, someone had overheard me. Not just someone, but the hostess of the party, in fact. It took some pretty fancy footwork to recover. In any case, even if you aren't overheard, it's a bad idea for two reasons: The people you are addressing may be good friends of other people at the party and may therefore be insulted, and it's simply too negative a comment for most people to accept as a compliment.

6. **Yes *and no*.** If the group you are trying to enter is made up of business peers who are no more powerful in your field than you, this is a fine, lighthearted piece of flattery. However, if the circle *does* contain "shakers and movers" of a much higher professional level than you, then this is a bad idea. Such a group must be entered carefully, in order not to draw too much attention to the fact that one of the lower echelon has had the audacity to join it.

7. **Yes.** This is the kind of Flattery Entrée that can work well (assuming you are approaching a circle of people who really have been laughing). It makes the people feel good without being threatening or too personal in any way, and it's believable, since you really can be drawn to people by their good energy. As with all openings, you will want to adapt it to your personality, using language that is comfortable for you.

Keep in mind that using flattery in an opening line and using it after you are involved in conversation are very different things. While it's often true that "flattery will get you everywhere," until you get to know what kind of people you are dealing with, you have to be very careful with the butter.

The Sophistication Test

There's no better way to find out what kind of person you're talking to than this, and it's also an excellent icebreaker. I use the Sophistication Test often, especially when I'm feeling out of my element. It's a quick, surefire method of figuring out what kind of subject matter, what tone, and what level of familiarity are appropriate. Please note that this opener must be directed to only one or two people at a time; if you are entering a larger group, use the Test on one person in the group. The question that I've found works best is: *"So how did you get here?"* (Be sure to smile.)

This question can obviously be taken many different ways, which is the whole purpose of the Test. If the person answers, "In a cab," you can relax a bit (although you might prepare to be a little bored); this person isn't going to throw you any curves and will probably stay more or less on the surface of things. If he or she replies, "Well, I knew the hostess's ex-husband, so I guess that's how I rated," you know you've got a fun person with whom you can kid around somewhat. Even, "How does *anyone* get here?" is good news; it's a sign of a witty conversationalist. But watch out for the guy or gal who says, "My father caught my mother on a good night"—this one's big trouble, and you've got to really hold on to your hat.

There are only two other types of responses, and both of them call for immediate escape. One of them is, "What business is it of yours?" and the other is, "I have no idea." The former signifies out-of-control hostility—a great detriment to mingling—and the latter could be evidence of mental impairment of some kind (or heavy-duty drugs).

You may want to concoct your own Sophistication Test question or use one of the ones listed here, but be sure whomever you use it on hasn't heard you giving the same Test to another guest. You don't want anyone to realize you are conducting preconversational research!

○ *"So what d'ya think?"*

○ *"How do you fit into this picture?"*

○ *"Well, what's your role in all this?"*

○ *"Hey—what's it all about anyway?"*

○ *"How's life treating you?"*

○ *"What's your story?"*

○ *"What's your connection here?"*

OPENING LINES FOR EVERY MOOD

If you choose not to use the Honest Approach, the Fade-in, the Flattery Entrée, or the Sophistication Test, you may want to employ one of the following opening lines. Along with my own tried-and-true favorites, which I have listed here, you may want to record your own pet lines. Most people can think of awesome opening lines—unfortunately, it's usually hours after the party has ended! Write them down for easy reference so that next time one will roll off your tongue like magic. Just remember to follow a few simple rules:

1. **Never, never, never (trust me) use "What do you do for a living?" as an opening line.** It's not only boring; it's also dangerous. The person may have just been fired or may be an

insurance broker, but whatever he is, unless it's something you find fascinating or know something about, it can be a real dead end. It also may seem to some people as if you are trying to find out if they are worth your time or how much money they make. In fact, once the person's told you what he does for a living, you are bound by the rules of courtesy to stick around and chat with him about it; you can't very well say, "Oh, sewage treatment, how interesting," and then turn around and leave.

2. **Those who mingle best mingle alone.** While you may have your *imaginary* "buddy" with you (if you're using the Buddy System), you don't want to actually mingle side by side with your mate or a friend—unless, of course, one of you knows most of the people there and is introducing the other one around. Occasionally you meet someone at the beginning of the party who is a little minglephobic, too, and it's tempting to go around the room together for the whole night; after all, it seems less scary that way. This is a no-no. It's too hard to assimilate into clusters when you are a pair; it can be threatening and, at the same time, it just looks wussy.

3. **Whatever words are coming out of your mouth, say them with strength and confidence.** If you find you're not getting anywhere with a certain line, but you can't understand why, try it one more time with a different inflection or a different accompanying facial expression on someone else. Above all, don't give up! Never forget, 90 percent of America has minglephobia, so you are not alone.

Don't be embarrassed to practice the following opening lines in the mirror (if that kind of thing appeals to you) or on a friend or loved one at home. Then, when you need them for mingling, the words will just flow naturally out of you.

Level One: The Risk-free Line

○ "This music reminds me of my childhood [high school days/college days]."

○ "How's life treating you?"

○ "So what was your day like today?"

○ "How do you know the host [hostess]?"

○ "Doesn't [name of host or hostess] look great tonight?"

○ "I just can't believe how beautiful/dark/noisy/crowded [et cetera] it is here; can you?"

○ "Isn't this [type of food you are eating or have tried] delicious?"

○ "I just love this place."

Level Two: The Playful Line

○ "Am I interrupting something confidential?"

○ "Excuse me, but what is that wonderful-looking thing you're eating [drinking]?"

○ "Please tell me someone is talking about a recent or upcoming vacation. I'm looking to relax vicariously."

○ "A little birdie told me this was the place to get the most up-to-date [name of your industry or professional area] news."

○ "Hello! I'm practicing my mingling tonight. How am I doing?"

Level Three: The Daring Line

○ *"OK, guys, what's the password over here?"*

○ *"I've been told that I should come and talk to you. I can't tell you who told me; I'm sworn to secrecy."*

○ *"If you're who I think you are, I've just heard the most wonderful things about you!" ("If you're who I think you are, I've just heard the most terrible things about you.")*

○ *"You're not going to believe this, but the hostess [host] seems to think we're related [knew each other in a past life]!"*

○ *"Every time I come to one of these things I wonder about the human race."*

○ *"Excuse me, but my friend and I were talking about mingling techniques and she bet me I couldn't walk up to you and immediately start talking—no, don't look at her! . . . Please just smile—that's good—and talk to me so I can win fifty dollars."*

○ *"You look so bored—so bored you must be very smart."*

Naturally, the success of these lines depends a lot on your delivery. Some of them require an ironic tone, some call for enthusiasm, some an air of puzzlement. Some of them will suit you better than others. Select the ones that seem most like something you would say, and remember that you can always alter them slightly to fit your own style. But don't be afraid to try something daring once in a while. It's not going to kill you, and it may *slay* them!

3 Now What? Tools and Rules for Continuing the Conversation

Now that you've chosen your first target group and have bravely uttered your opening line, you may be wondering, *Now what? What happens after the opening?* Well, you've got three options:

1. You can hang about silently, listening to the other people in the group talk, satisfied that you've actually pulled off an opening (in other words, stop mingling).

2. You can exit immediately upon completing the opening gambit, using one of the techniques described in chapter 4.

3. You can segue smoothly into a conversation with one or more of the people with whom you are now standing.

Obviously, the most rewarding choice, from a mingling standpoint, is option 3, which is, for many people, the hardest part of the mingling experience. Getting into a group is one thing; holding your own in that group is another. Even a smashingly successful opening line is only the beginning, like getting accepted into college. Now you actually have to *go* to college. In fact, many people are just as terror stricken after a successful opening line as after one that flubs, even though they presumably now have the other person's attention and everything is A-OK. A good response to your opening may give you a temporary high, but then your minglephobia usually sets in again. *Oh my God,* you think frantically to yourself, *what do I talk about with this person?* Don't worry. This chapter should give you enough ammunition so you won't end up tongue-tied, red faced, or sweaty palmed ever again. It's much easier to find things to say than we have been conditioned to think. There's a whole world of subject matter out there, and there are some easy methods to keep a variety of topics at your fingertips.

But first of all, let's address the worst-case scenario.

RECOVERING FROM A FLUBBED OPENING

Sometimes your opening line will fall flat on the ground and just lie there, dead. Don't be disheartened; this can be demoralizing, but it happens to everyone at one time or another. There are things you can do:

○ **Pretend it never happened.** Simply start over with another opening line. For example, suppose you chose the Fade-in entrance, but you're noticed before you get a chance to listen to the conversation and complete the maneuver. Everyone has stopped talking and is looking at you. *Don't panic.* You can switch immediately to the Honest Approach, the Flattery Entrée, or the Sophistication Test (this one's harder with a large group but still doable) or deliver one of the opening lines you've memorized. It's really not difficult to move quickly to another opening gambit, and it's important to know that it is not unusual to use more than one opening. The essential thing is not to lose your confidence. Don't let it be known that you are disappointed your opening missed its mark. The survival fantasies can really help at a time like this.

○ **Be unapologetic.** Let's say you used the line (see p. 26) "Am I interrupting something confidential?" and you get the number-one killer reaction from the group: They exchange looks with each other that say, *What a bimbo!* and offer no verbal response of any kind. In other words, the Silent Treatment. Now, once in a while someone may respond to this particular line with a, "Yes, actually you are," in which case you should apologize politely and move on. But in the case of the Silent Meanies, I suggest you laugh (if you can, or at least smile) and say, "Well! I can see that's the last time I try that line!" or smile more widely and say, "I guess I did!" It indicates that you can't be intimidated and that you know you haven't done anything wrong. You've merely stumbled accidentally into a patch of boors.

○ **Make something up.** In the same situation as in the last scenario, for example, say, "Look, I know that sounded rather odd, but I just had the most unsettling experience; I introduced myself to some people over there, as [name of host] suggested, and they told me they were having a private conversation, *thank you very much,* and they didn't want to be disturbed. So I thought I'd better check this time!" Or, if you've approached someone from behind, you can always use the old standard: "Oh, excuse me! I really did think you were somebody else."

○ **Be funny.** You really have to be careful with humor, which is something I'll address later in this chapter. But for some people, having their opening bomb is so devastating that the only way for them to keep up their confidence and go on is to strike back with a funny line, as a comedian does with hecklers. Take the same example of the "confidential" line and the worst-case, icy reaction. You might be able to win them with, "Are you going to talk to me or am I under arrest?" Or how about, "Has the stock market crashed?" or, "What? Is my face purple or something?" You might even try, "Ah, pardonnez-moi. Vous ne parlez pas anglais? . . . Parlez-vous francais? . . . Espagnol? . . . " Or, "Haven't you people ever heard of an opening line?"

○ **Retreat.** If the response is really as hostile as the extreme case I've suggested, your best move may be just to leave these bozos in the dust, unless there's some pressing reason to try further (for example, if one of them happens to be an important business contact). Try someone else, and use a different line, at least for a while. Some lines are just wrong, for some parties, and some lines may be ill suited to you. Don't let one bad experience keep you from trying again.

CAREER TALK: YES OR NO?

Assuming your opening succeeds or that you recover your balance sufficiently after a flubbed opening, you're still going to need some ready topics for when the conversation lags (or stops completely; I don't want to frighten you, but this may happen some if you're an inexperienced mingler). Ideally, you want each interaction to last at least ten minutes—that's optimum mingle time—and usually the dialogue surrounding the opening will last no longer than one or two minutes. So what do you do when the fervor of the opening dies down and the awkward cone of silence begins to descend?

Most people automatically leap right into, "So what do you do for a living?" or more often, "What do *you* do?" as if their own occupation has already been the subject of much exciting deliberation at the party.

Please believe me when I say that this is not a good idea. When and where to talk "career-ese" is a debatable issue, but I do not recommend it until and unless you have already established a rapport with the person(s). Many people will disagree with me on this. After all, this advice goes against a golden rule of conversation that has been drilled into our heads and that, for the most part, serves us very well: People like it when you ask them to talk about themselves. This is, of course, basically true, and if you can't think of anything else, asking about someone's career certainly may be preferable to stuttering or fainting. In other words, it's a perfectly acceptable default position. But you should be aware of the possible consequences and pitfalls:

○ The person's occupation may be something really **boring** and something he or she just loves to talk about—for hours. This can be no fun at all and makes you susceptible to what I call the Glaze-out, which is similar to being hypnotized, except that it's not relaxing or particularly good for you. It's almost impossible to mingle when you're in the grip of the Glaze-out. When it happens to me, I find that I can't concentrate at all on what's being said (much less say anything myself except, "Uh-huh") and that I usually become transfixed by a small section of the person's face.

○ The person's occupation may be something **repulsive** to you. He could be a proctologist, or a mortician, or a hair transplant technician, or a political operative from the *other* party, and what are you going to say then? A friend of mine who is a vegan told me about the time she introduced herself to an interesting-looking man at a large party and then right away asked him what he did.

"I'm a butcher," he said, smiling proudly.

"Oh . . . ah . . . I . . . how interesting," my friend managed to reply, blanching.

"Yep. Best butcher in the city. In business for thirty-six years." He went on to describe in gruesome detail what his day had entailed, involving a delivery for the holidays: two dozen turduckens (turkeys stuffed with ducks stuffed with chickens) and some wild rabbit. "Say, what's the matter?" he asked after several minutes. "You look a little green."

"Excuse me, won't you?" my friend finally squeaked. That was the end of that conversation. Her hasty exit would have been much less embarrassing if she had talked to the man a little longer before she brought up professions. As it was, it seemed as if she introduced herself and then immediately bolted. Remember that when you bring up this subject you actually do not have any idea what subject you are bringing up!

○ The person's answer may be something **depressing** (or embarrassing). Let's say you've used flattery as your entrance. You're all smiles and cheer from delivering the compliment, and then you ask, "What do you do?" Suppose the person says with a quiver in his or her lip, "Well, actually, I'm between jobs at the moment, and I, well, today I thought I had gotten this job, but . . . I didn't." This isn't a total disaster, of course, but it's not the greatest thing in the world to work with, as you almost have to come back with, "Oh, I'm sorry to hear that. What field are you in?" and you're going to have some real downer minutes before you can change the subject. The answer could also be something that's depressing to *you*. The person could work with drug-addicted babies, and while that is a compelling subject and a noble job, you might not want to find yourself in that kind of conversation right off the bat.

The point is, you are playing Conversational Roulette with the career query, and it could leave you in the position of wanting out desperately before you've said more than two sentences. And beware: *The sooner it is after you have started the conversation, the harder it is to escape*. Also, if you pose this question to more than one person, it often means the destruction of the group as a unit. One person answers, and because of the nature of the dialogue, some or all of the others can use your entrance into this subject to escape, which they will do, especially if they've already discovered the person is a snooze. Now you're really stuck, because it is much harder to escape from one person than from many. At the very least, you've lessened your chances of having witty repartee or a back-and-forth among the whole group you've just taken great pains to enter. So before you jump into career talk, find out a little more about this person (or people) first. *Note:* The Sophistication Test sometimes works even better as a second line than it does as a first.

If you *must* talk careers right away, try a career semiquery. For instance, say, "Did you come here directly from work?" That way, it opens up the field for career talk, but you have a little safety zone to protect yourself in case something dreadful happens.

As far as career talk goes, there are more exceptions to the rule than in any other area of mingling. For one thing, none of these warnings apply if you are at a specific business function such as a company party or your industry's annual convention. Also, there are many situations in which you can tell right away—for a wide variety of reasons—that it is a safe question and one you are expected to ask. At any rate, in most cases it's certainly not the worst thing you can do, by any means. I'm merely urging you to remember the dangers and consider your options before you commit to this. There's so much more to talk about, so many other ways to really enjoy mingling!

AN ABCEDARY FOR THOSE
AT A LOSS FOR WORDS

What *do you* talk about, now that you're standing there with nothing but a blank computer screen in your mind and you can't seem to find the button to make anything appear? We've all been in this position, where fifteen seconds of silence can seem like an hour. Even though you are probably not alone in your terror, as obviously no one else is saying anything, either, it is undeniably your responsibility to get things going, since you are the one who has approached *them*.

We all know there are literally millions of subjects from which to choose: observations about the party or about current events; questions about people's background or connection to the host or hostess; and, if it's a business affair, remarks about whatever may be new or exciting in your profession. The problem is how to pull something out of the air when you're stumped. So before we go any further, I'm going to offer you a very simple way—a trick, really—to think of a good topic.

When you were a child, did you ever memorize things for a history or geography class by using word-association games? My mother was crazy about this study technique, and I can remember listening to her coaching my brother with, "What's the capital of Maryland? It's such a *merry land* that everyone in it gets *an apple*. Annapolis!" Sound ridiculous? Maybe, but it worked, and while this process might not suit everyone, you'll never draw a blank again if you can master this handy miniature mingling manual for the subject-starved minglephobic.

Here's how to use it: After you have completed your opening, if you now know the name of the person or one of the people in the group, use the first letter of his or her name to remind you of one of the twenty-six key topics that follow. For example, if you've just met someone named Alice, think, *A*, which should lead you to think of the word "art." If you don't know anyone's name yet, use the color of someone's jacket or blouse to pick a letter (e.g., blue, *B*). Use hair or eye color or the last word that was said to you. It really doesn't matter what you use to select the letter; you can simply start with *A* at the beginning of the night and work your way through the alphabet, if you want. The important thing is speed. It has to look as if you are one of those people who have a fascinating mind, able to leap from one interesting subject to another. You can deliver the line in the form it is given in the Abcedary, or you can use any of the following lead-ins:

○ *"I was just saying to someone that . . ."*

○ *"It's interesting how . . ."*

○ *"Have you ever noticed . . ." (the Andy Rooney lead-in)*

○ *"What do **you** think about . . ." (my favorite: It implies the topic has already been a great success)*

○ *"I can't believe . . ."*

LETTER	SAMPLE LINES
A is for Art	*"Don't you think when Steve works a room it's an art form?"*
	"Look at all these people; I like looking at people more than any art in any museum I've ever seen!"
	"Do you suppose the art hanging on a wall genuinely affects the conversation of the people beside that wall?"
B is for Baby	*"I can't believe how many babies there are now at parties."*
	"What do you think a party like this would look like to a baby?"
	"When I get home I'm just going to baby myself."

(continued)

LETTER	SAMPLE LINES
C is for Cat	*"Did you see a cat in here?"* *"Are you a cat person or a dog person?"* *"Can you help me out? I'm trying to decide what to name my cat."*
D is for Danger	*"Don't you think it's dangerous to put all these [name of your business or profession] people in the same room?"* *"There's danger in the air tonight."* *"What is the international sign for danger?"*
E is for Energy	*"The energy is really good at this party, isn't it?"* *"I don't know why, but I'm very low-/high-energy tonight."* *"How much energy do you think it took to make this party possible?"*
F is for Food	*"Have you tried the food?"* *"Don't let me have any more food!"* *"Everything in our lives really revolves around food, doesn't it?"*
G is for Glowing	*"Don't you think [name of host or hostess] is glowing tonight?"* *"I think this party is a glowing success; don't you?"* *"Does it look to you like this food is kind of glowing?"*
H is for Host (Hostess)	*"So how do you know our host [hostess]?"* *"Look at Susan! She always was a natural-born hostess!"* *"Is there someone hosting this thing or did it just happen somehow?"*

LETTER	SAMPLE LINES
I is for Ice	*"Is it cold in here? My fingers are like ice."* *"So many people drink wine now, no one ever has to worry about running out of ice."* *"Have you ever wondered where the saying 'break the ice' comes from? And after we break the ice, what if we fall in?"*
J is for Jewelry	*"What a great ring [pair of earrings, watch, necklace]!"* *"Is that an engagement [wedding] ring?"* *"If I had known it was going to be such a fancy party, I'd have worn my tiara."*
K is for Kill	*"Isn't this cheesecake [pâté/punch/dip] killer?"* *"My feet are killing me."* *"I could just kill for this apartment [furniture, china, garden]."*
L is for Laugh	*"Tell me something funny; I could use a laugh."* *"Do you think the best parties are always the ones where you laugh the most?"* *"What this party needs is a laugh track!"*
M is for Magic	*"There's magic in the air tonight."* *"I always wish I could do magic, so that when I first met people I could pull a quarter out of their ear or something."* *"Wouldn't it be great if when the party was over one could magically transport oneself home to bed?"*
N is for Noise	*"Hey, I hear you're making a big noise in the industry!"*

(continued)

LETTER	SAMPLE LINES

"Do you think the noise level in here has any true correlation with the fun level?"

"What do you suppose makes humans think the noise they make is any more important than the noise anything else makes?"

O is for Old

"I can't believe how old I feel!"

"You know, you remind me of a very old friend of mine."

"I'm getting too old for this kind of thing."

P is for Practice

"I need practice talking to people I don't know."

"Don't you think they should throw a practice party before the real one?"

"That food looks delicious. I think I'll practice for when I go off my diet."

Q is for Quiz

"Someone just told me I looked quizzical. Do I look quizzical to you?"

"Please don't quiz me on any of your names, because I can never remember names."

"OK, I am administering a pop quiz. Name three of the things you have just eaten off the buffet table."

R is for Real Estate

"In what part of town do you live?"

"Isn't this a great [scary, funky, fun, cool] neighborhood?"

"I'd love to own a house [apartment, condo, building, boat, convention hall] like this one."

S is for Sun

"I feel as if I have talked about everything under the sun tonight."

LETTER	SAMPLE LINES

"What a relief to talk to you. There's a guy here who thinks the sun rises and sets with him!"

"You seem to have a fairly sunny disposition. Or am I about to get burnt?"

T is for Toes

"Every time I come to one of these, someone steps on my toes."

"You seem like someone who can really keep me on my toes!"

"I'm this close to taking off my shoes and letting my toes roam free."

U is for Utopia

"Would your version of Utopia have parties in it?"

"This party is a virtual Utopia!"

"I have a friend who says Utopia is a place with no people. He obviously never met you."

V is for Vocabulary

"Have you ever wondered just how many words there are in your vocabulary?"

"Tell me something unusual; I'm trying to improve my vocabulary."

"In this business it's nice to meet someone with the same vocabulary."

W is for Winner

"Do you think of yourself as a winner, a loser, or a tie-er?"

"Hey, did you hear about [name of business associate]? She [he] sure turned out to be a winner!"

(continued)

LETTER　　　　　SAMPLE LINES

"Tonight I feel like life's just one big door prize and I'm the winner."

X is for Xerox　*"You're not talking to the real me tonight; this is just a Xerox."*

"I hope you'll bear with me. I've been repeating myself so much tonight I feel like a Xerox machine!"

"I'd love to have a Xerox copy of the conversation I just had with the people across the room."

Y is for Yell　*"I'm glad we don't [I wish we didn't] have to yell."*

"If I lose your interest, just yell."

"You know, sometimes at affairs like this one, I get the strangest urge to stand up on a chair and yell real loud."

Z is for Zoo　*"Boy, what a zoo!"*

"It was almost impossible to get here; it was such a zoo out there!"

"Have you ever thought that maybe we're really in some alien zoo and just don't know it?"

Please note: The sample lines I've provided are merely examples. You can adapt the topics to your own sensibility and style, of course. Or, particularly if you're the kind of person who always thinks of great things to talk about before and after a party but never during, you may prefer to substitute some of your own mingling topics— ones that are easily accessible to you.

Also, this mingling crib sheet is purposely designed for observations or questions of a fairly nonpersonal nature. This is because, for the best mingling experience, you need to remain in control and, ideally, ready to move off to another group. Specific questions about personal life, while easy for most people to think of, usually commit you to an involved discourse with one person in the group. Using a little imagination will pay off in the long run!

TRIED-AND-TRUE TRICKS OF THE TRADE

Name-Tag Tips

I went through a period in my life when I refused to wear the sticky, annoying labels we are all encouraged to don at many business, pseudobusiness, alumnae, or association affairs. After all, if you're wearing a bright blue or red tag that announces: "HELLO MY NAME IS——," you can feel kind of dumb saying it as well; it's almost as if you're reading your name tag aloud to the other person. I used to have this nightmarish fantasy that someone would yell back at me, "Hey, I can read, stupid!"

I've mellowed on the subject of name tags since then. Now I believe you should wear them if they are provided—with the exception of the ones that pin on. (Call me fussy, but I don't think people should be asked to put holes in their clothing in the name of socializing, unless they're wearing burlap or something disposable.) Even though name tags are a silly mingling crutch, I have found that it is better to go ahead and wear them, if for no other reason than it makes you part of the group. Also—you never know—someone at the party may have been told to talk to you because you're fabulous or brilliant (or available!) and that person may be darting in and out of clusters of people reading tags and hoping to find you. If you are not wearing a name tag, you could miss the best conversation of your life.

However, if you are bored by the prospect of conventional name-tag practice, here are some suggestions to liven things up:

○ **Wear it in an interesting place.** I've seen tags on lapels (sideways), purses or briefcases, hats, the lower part of a jacket—even sleeves. Women often choose an alternative to the chest because they feel uncomfortable having people look pointedly at that part of the body. As long as you have chosen to wear a name tag, you may as well get the most out of it conversationally. And if your tag is in an interesting—even original—place, it can be an icebreaker.

○ **Write something else instead of your name.** This is admittedly kind of silly, but what's wrong with silly? You could write something like: "Guess!" or, "You'd never be able to pronounce it," or maybe, "Don't you hate name tags?" I've even heard of taping on a bar code in place of a name. You'd be surprised how many people enjoy seeing something out of the ordinary. *Caution:* Don't go too far. Never, never write something that is crude or impolite in any way (this includes remarks that are sexist, racist, etc.). If you have to ask yourself, *Is this offensive?* don't do it.

○ **Write your name and draw an arrow pointing toward your face.** This is a little cutesy, but some people like cutesy.

○ **Use punctuation.** The obvious one is an exclamation mark. A question mark may be a good choice for an intellectual crowd. Underlining can be distinctive yet conservative. And for the serious business gathering: your last name first, then a comma, then your first name, better still your first name underneath (in parentheses).

○ **Write illegibly.** Scrawl or scratch your name so that no one can possibly decipher it. This can serve as an interesting test to see who will admit they can't read it and who won't. When someone does comment on it, you can have some conversation starters ready, such as: "It's my own personal protest against name tags," or, "I always wanted to be a doctor, but I never got past Bad Handwriting 101."

Whether or not you choose to employ any of the preceding un-subtle name-tag tricks, there are a couple of things to keep in mind when mingling among name-tag wearers. If you are going with the straight name-tag approach, be sure to write clearly in large letters so that people don't have to stick their faces into your chest to read your name. Also, it's best not to look at people's tags until you have ap-proached them or the group they are in. It's very rude to be seen check-ing out the tags of everyone in the room, unless you can appear to be on a dedicated mission looking for someone specific. If you do glance at people's tags while you pass by, do not make eye contact with any of them, or it will be as if you are saying, *I don't like your name; I don't like your face; I'm going to look elsewhere for conversational partners.* Also, when you enter into a conversation with someone, it's best to be defi-nite with regard to the tag; either look at it and comment on it or don't look at it (at least not so the person notices).

A great name-tag trick is to glance quickly at the tag without letting the wearer see you. Then wait a few minutes and slip the wearer's name into the conversation as if you're old chums ("Well, Bob . . ."). This simple trick, when done well, seems to impress most people.

The Interview

A lot of people insist that the true secret to social success is simply to ask a lot of questions about the other person. Indubitably, showing interest in others is the golden rule of all interaction; no matter how many tricks you learn, nothing will work if you are not interested in the person you're talking to. It is, however, an oversimplification to say that all you have to do is ask questions. (If it were that easy there wouldn't be millions of Web sites and articles about how to talk to people and you probably wouldn't be reading this book!) For one thing, exactly *what* questions are you supposed to ask a stranger? Most people can't come up with anything when they are feeling nervous, and it can be hard to know what kinds of things are too intrusive to ask and what aren't.

More important, merely asking questions may not result in the give-and-take that is essential to lively conversation. You need to get the ball rolling. Obviously a willingness to listen to the other person is a virtue, yet ultimately conversations when you are mingling should be like a volleyball game, with everyone participating equally. For some people, interviewing can actually be a hiding technique—if you continue asking other people about themselves, you never have to share anything about *you*. In addition, the Interview technique can upset the integrity of a group, because you can only interview one person at a time. If you walk up to Sharon and Emily and start interviewing Sharon, Emily will quickly go elsewhere.

Given these provisos, interviewing someone can be a perfectly fine way to proceed. If you are standing with only one person and it's what comes naturally to you, then go ahead and conduct an Interview. Hopefully the other person will turn the tables and interview *you* after a while. If you find yourself faced with a very shy person, the Interview style is sometimes the only way you can think of to try to draw him out.

So . . . go ahead and pretend you're Barbara Walters. Ask lots of questions—preferably questions that require more than a yes or no answer. (I do *not* recommend you use the Charlie Rose style of interviewing: that is, asking questions that go on and on until neither one of you can remember where you began!) Start with asking what connection the person has to the event and let his answer lead you to the next question. The best questions for drawing out a fellow minglephobe are questions involving superlatives, such as, "Who was your most difficult client?" or, "What is the longest time you ever spent negotiating a deal?" Have your next question ready as soon as his reply is out of his mouth; his answers are not bound to be very lengthy. As you ask the questions, watch his face carefully for any signs of life. If you see a flicker, you may have hit upon a conversational hot spot, and you will want to pursue that line of questioning.

Note: If interviewing someone doesn't work or if you get tired of it, try flattering him. It's always a good idea when dealing with insecure people (or secure people, for that matter) to flatter them, especially in areas where they may feel the weakest. So say to him, "I'm so glad you're here! It's nice when one meets a like-minded person at these things." If the person doesn't open up after that one, then you've done your best and it may be time to move on. Remember, a serious minglephobe can drain you of your energy, because you will be doing the work for both of you.

Playing a Game

Here's a really fun way to keep things going but not dig too deeply. It takes a little courage, but you'll be pleasantly surprised at how well most people respond. I use this technique quite often, though I never realized it until several years ago, when I was spending a weekend with a friend in Stockbridge, Massachusetts. He and I had been arguing good-naturedly all day about whether my jacket was orange or red. (He thought it was red; I *knew* it was orange.) That night we went to a fairly large dance where I knew no one. My friend immediately melted into the crowd, leaving me to fend for myself. Never being much of one to stand alone in a corner, I marched right up to a group of people and entered it, using the Honest Approach. After the introductions were finished, there was that inevitable moment of silence; my intrusion had disturbed the conversational flow.

Suddenly I had an idea. As if it were plaguing my mind, I asked the group at large, "What color would you call this jacket?" They were a little taken aback but intrigued. They each answered in turn, and I noted that the two men said "red" and the woman "orange." This led to a quite interesting conversation about color perception and sex difference, and, as anyone knows, once you start talking about the differences between the sexes, you're home free.

The great thing about Playing a Game is it is such a fluid mingling technique. It facilitates bringing new members into the group ("Hey, come over here; we want to ask you something!") as well as exiting a group ("I'll be back; I want some other opinions!"). Also, you get to know people by how they play the game, which is a more relaxing, easier—and sometimes more revealing—way to find out about someone. Game playing is one of my absolutely *most recommended* tactics; it epitomizes the true spirit of mingling!

Here are some sample game lines to explore. However, you'll definitely discover that once you use this device once or twice, you will begin to invent your own. Don't ever forget your primary goal (even if you are at a business function): Have fun!

○ *"What color would you say this [——] is?"*

○ *"Guess what my nickname was as a child?"* [*"Let me guess your childhood nickname."*]

○ *"I'm into regional accents. Guess where I grew up?"* [*"Let me guess where you grew up."*]

○ *"Close your eyes. Now tell me what I'm wearing [. . . what color eyes I have]."*

○ *"Tell me three things about your company and I'll guess what company it is."*

Party Favors: The Helpless Hannah Ploy

Brace yourself, because this is probably going to offend some people. All I can say is that I've seen this method employed all my life, by both children and adults, and it works. It's kind of a knock-down, drag-out way of mingling; but I must confess that even I have used it on occasion, with spectacular success. If done well, the Helpless Hannah Ploy can make you the star of the party.

Ready? Think of yourself as a damsel in distress (or a knight in need) and the other guests as your rescuers. If you put people in the role of helping you, it: (1) gives them a purpose, (2) flatters them, (3) leaves you in control, and (4) most important, gives you something to say.

My favorite version of this technique is getting someone to "protect me" from someone else. For example, after my opening, I'll say something like, "Listen. There's someone here I'm desperately trying to avoid—I can't tell you who it is, but you'd be doing me a big favor if, when you see me doing this," and I show the person some subtle hand or eye signal, "you'd just come over and check up on me if you can." Naturally, people want to know who it is and why I am avoiding him or her. I won't be able to tell them, of course, having made the whole thing up, but it makes for great conversation. Also, usually what happens is that people will keep checking up on me to see if I need protection even if I don't give the signal (which I usually don't). If you tell a few different sets of people this story, you can get a big rush all evening, and everyone will wonder what your secret power is.

Another—often more subtle—way to play the Helpless Hannah is to ask as many people as you can to help you obtain information. You can say to person X that you heard an important business contact was going to be present and would X mind letting you know when the contact arrives. If X doesn't know the contact, you can still ask X to keep her ears open for anyone who does. You can mention to person Y that later on in the evening you will need a ride home and if Y should happen to meet anyone who he knows is going in your direction, to please let you know. When introduced to person Z, you can ask Z for yet a different piece of information or use one of the ones you used before.

It doesn't matter what information you request. The important part of this gambit is that when X, Y, or Z says he or she doesn't have the answer to your question, you say, "Well, do me a favor and let me know if you *do* find out." That way, if you query enough people, some of them will return throughout the evening to report to you. Getting people involved with you in this manner is your insurance against ever being a wallflower.

The other, more "Scarlett O'Hara" form of the Helpless Hannah Ploy is asking people to get you *things*. You'll need to invent a reason you can't get the thing yourself, which can be tricky and can occasionally backfire, but if you are able to pull it off, this can serve an additional purpose: getting rid of somebody. Here's how it works:

Betty has just begun to talk to John and Tom. From the responses to the Sophistication Test she has just used ("How did you get here?") she senses Tom is more interesting than John. The conversation has died down now and all three people are beginning to get that furtive look signaling the early stages of minglephobia until Betty says to John, "Would you mind doing me a big favor and getting me a glass of wine? There's someone over near the bar I'd really rather not talk to." John has no choice, really, but to acquiesce. So off he goes, leaving Betty with the more interesting Tom, at least for the moment. Betty can use many other excuses in playing this "fetch and carry" form of Helpless Hannah. She can say she has to wait near the phone; she can say she doesn't want to lose her place in line for food or for the powder room.

When performing this technique always be very grateful if and when the person returns with the requested item, the information you wanted, or to see if you are OK. If you have several people protecting you, several people getting you information, and another bunch of people bringing you things, it can really liven up your mingling experience. People will be coming up to you constantly, and you can end up with an absolute throng around you.

There are some serious risks involved with the Helpless Hannah approach that I'm sure are fairly obvious. Don't overdo the avoiding line—people will think you are paranoid or a snob—and never, ever indicate a real-live guest as the object of your avoidance (even if it's true). I did this once, in an effort to make my Helpless Hannah a little more believable. After asking for protection, I pointed a finger surreptitiously at the back of a man standing at the bar. To my horror, the woman I had been talking to turned a cold eye on me and said with suspicion, "That's my husband!"

Room with a View

If you are at a fairly large party, you might want to try using this device, which is low-risk but still marvelously effective. This is especially useful for those times when you are feeling very nonwitty and you have just begun to talk to either one or two people (this strategy works best in a small group).

What you do is point out (subtly, please!) someone else at the party, preferably someone across the room, and make an observation. People love to talk about other people, and this way you can have a very nonthreatening verbal exchange and find out a little about whom you're talking to before you decide to enter into more personal territory. Here are some lines you might try:

○ *"Did you see that woman over there? Isn't that the wildest hat you've ever seen?"*

○ *"Look at old J.B. I've never seen him look so happy; have you?"*

○ *"See that man over by the door? Do you know who he is? I think I've met him somewhere, but I can't remember."*

○ *"Is that Joyce's daughter? She's so tall now."*

○ *"Have you talked to that person over there? Is she a friend of yours? I found her very interesting [funny, mysterious, etc.]."*

The lines you use, of course, will depend on what you can notice about people at a specific party. If you're at a Halloween party you can have a field day! *Warning:* I am not condoning vicious gossip. It is vital to remember that you are not, under any circumstances, to say anything nasty about the object of your voyeurism. Doing so can get you into more hot water than I have space to talk about here.

Using Clichés

Just because I am overly fond of clichés myself doesn't mean that I necessarily recommend their use for others. But there actually is a good way, in conversations, to use clichés effectively.

Irony is the key. The following lines, executed with enough irony, sarcasm, or just plain whimsy, can become your staples:

○ *"Haven't I seen you somewhere before?"*

○ *"Come here often?"*

○ *"What's a girl like you doing in a place like this?"*

○ *"What's your sign?"*

○ *"We've got to stop meeting like this."*

When exaggerated, these standards can work as openers or as second or third lines (better irony results if they are *not* first lines), and they also serve as a sort of Sophistication Test. Best of all, they're easy to remember!

About Eye Contact

When it comes to being a good mingler, subject matter isn't every-thing. The wittiest line, if it's delivered while you're looking at the floor or someone's crotch, is worthless. Here are a few tried-and-true tips about how your eyes—the most important mingling asset you possess—should behave:

○ **Look straight at anyone who is speaking to you.** I mean this literally; that is, look into the person's eyes during those periods when sound is actually coming out of that person's mouth. Eyes are extremely powerful, and as long as you are looking at the other person, you can be in la-la land and still appear to be listening.

○ **Use the time when *you* are speaking to look away.** Certainly if you are having a very intense discussion, you may be too spellbound to want to do this, and that's OK. But it's a fact of human communication that while you are speaking you can turn your eyes anywhere else in the room and still seem totally involved in the current conversation. This works as long as when the other person resumes speaking, you immediately make eye contact with him or her again. *Note:* With close friends, the rules of eye contact change. Both people can stare at the ceiling and the conversation still works.

I encourage you to practice your eye roaming because it is es-sential, if you want to become an expert mingler, to be aware of what is happening around you. First, your escape will be a lot easier if you know where you want to escape to, and for that you have to scope out the room. Second, there are techniques you may want to slide into at a moment's notice—the Helpless Hannah, a Room with a View—that necessitate keen peripheral vision.

○ **Use your eyes for emphasis.** If you learn to use your eyes well, it's almost as good as having a million-dollar smile. Many people, in their frenzy to keep up a dialogue, forget that the eyes are the true center of communication. You can use eye contact to pick someone out of a group and let him know you want to talk to him one-on-one. You can use your eyes, along with a very slight nod, to point out something in the room. You can use eye expressions instead of words, either because words fail you or just because your eyes can say it better: Roll your eyes ("Oh, I *know!*"), shut your eyes (Oh, how horrible!"), blink your eyes fast ("I'm trying to take this in, but it's all very strange"), or raise your eyebrows ("Oh, really?"). I happen to be one of those people who can raise one eyebrow, a very dramatic gesture and very effective ("Oh, *come on* now!"). Practice these eye expressions in the mirror; they can not only save you when you don't know what to say but also add to your general conversational charm.

The Dot-Dot-Dot Plot

I have used, and needed, this trick at almost every party I have ever attended. I rely on this technique because, I am embarrassed to confess, if I am not terribly interested in what the other person is saying my mind tends to wander a little bit. This can be *very* awkward at a party. Suddenly I'll find that someone has been talking to me and I have no idea what she has been talking about. And now she's *stopped* talking and I am expected to respond. The feeling of panic is exactly like that you got when you were called on in class when you'd been daydreaming. And even if you happen to be better at staying focused than I am, you will invariably get caught in this situation at some time or other, if only because the hot roast beef or a hot guy just caught your eye for a moment and distracted you. Getting caught not paying attention at a party when someone is speaking directly to you is a *serious* mingling faux pas. I still experience that split-second rush of adrenaline when it happens. But then I remember: *Have no fear; the Dot-Dot-Dot Plot is here!*

When you "come to" in this situation, you almost always are aware of the last few words the person has said. It's just that without any other clues you're lost. What you can do is use those few words any way you can and then employ the all-important, all-powerful pause. The people in the group are not going to suspect you haven't been listening (unless you tell them) if you *have maintained eye contact*, per the instructions above. Keep in mind that everyone is busy thinking about how well they themselves are communicating. So as long as you give them a, "You mean . . . ," or a, "So what you're saying is . . . ," or, "You're kidding . . . ," they'll go right on talking.

I promise that you are going to be surprised at how well this works. It's scary the first time you try it; it sort of feels like stepping off the edge of a cliff, but when you find out how successful and powerful the pause is, you'll be astounded. One of the most popular closing techniques taught at sales seminars is something called the Pause Close. It's based on the same principle as the Dot-Dot-Dot Plot: Human beings are very uncomfortable with pauses and will automatically do anything to end them. The Dot-Dot-Dot Plot is really very simple to use; in a way, it is just a glorified version of "Uh-huh." *Note:* The more you are able to work the last few words you may have heard into your delivery, the more convincing it will be.

If you are successful and no one ever finds out you hadn't been paying attention, start listening with all your might.

○ *"You mean . . ."*

○ *"So what you're saying is . . ."*

○ *"Hmm. I don't know much about that kind of thing. . . ."*

○ *"You can say that again. . . ."*

○ *"Wow. . . ."*

○ *"You're kidding—really? . . ."*

○ *"You can't be serious. . . ."*

○ *"Amazing. . . ."*

○ *"That's so cool. . . ."*

○ *"I love hearing that kind of thing. . . ."*

○ *"Then what happened? . . ."*

The Echo Chamber

A close cousin to the Dot-Dot-Dot Plot, the Echo Chamber is not particularly inspired or witty, but it is a great contingency strategy. It is for those times when you are completely aware of what is being said to you, but for some reason your social machinery is on the blink. Use this technique when you are very tired or suffering from general brain freeze. It's a bit of an inane way to converse, so it's best to use it just for resting, like putting the controls of the plane on automatic pilot temporarily. Here's an example:

OTHER PERSON: . . . So, I told Susie she had to choose: soccer or the school play.

YOU: Right. Soccer or the school play.

OP: But then of course, her best friend Harriet is doing *both*. So now of course Susie thinks *she* should be able to do both. It's a mess.

YOU: God, you're right. What a mess.

OP: But you know, she has to learn that just because the other kids get to do something, that doesn't mean she does. Life doesn't work that way.

YOU: That's for sure. Life doesn't work that way.

Alright, so it's not an earth-shattering exchange. But remember, this is a fallback tactic, meant for temporary use only. *Note:* It helps to smile and/or laugh during the Echo Chamber. Otherwise people will suspect you are not really participating in the conversation.

The Funny Thing About Humor

The funny thing about humor is how often people try to be funny and how rarely they are. A lot of people see a bright, gaily laughing group and think laughter must be the key to success and therefore they've got to be funny. But there's nothing worse than humor badly executed while mingling. Don't let this happen to you:

"Hiya, stranger!! Hee-hee! Want to hear a funny story? Ha-ha! This is so funny, it's going to kill you!! Hee-hee! A man walks up to a . . . this is so funny; just wait . . . a man walks up to a bar . . . ha-ha . . . I mean, a woman walks up to a bar, no, a woman walks *into* a bar, hee-hee, no . . . this is so great, it's going to kill you; wait . . . hey, wait a minute; where are you going?"

This is an extreme case, of course, but you'd be surprised how many people turn to humor when they shouldn't—especially when they are nervous. When a joke works, the rewards are great; when it doesn't, it's a disaster. Humor is very subjective, and its success or failure depends as much on the audience as grapevines do on the climate. I'm not about to try to teach anyone how to be funny. But here are a few basic guidelines:

○ **Don't *try* to be funny.** If you're trying too hard, it won't be funny. Be aware that you may try overly hard when you are feeling insecure.

○ **Don't tell jokes.** Unless you enter a group that is already telling jokes or the joke you have to tell is a proven success *and* is relevant to the situation (the day's events, the party itself, etc.), it is best to stay away from joke telling. There are few things worse than when your joke bombs in front of strangers (ask any comic).

○ **Don't announce in advance that your personal anecdote is going to be funny.**

○ **Don't make your stories inordinately long.**

○ **Don't touch people to encourage them to laugh.** It's as if you are saying to the person, *Hey, did you hear me, did you get it?*

○ **Don't laugh too much yourself.** In fact, it's best not to laugh at all, at least not until other people do. A big smile is enough.

○ **Don't make fun of other people.** If you must make fun of someone to get a laugh, let it be yourself.

○ **Don't make off-color remarks.** Humor of a sexual or crude nature should be avoided unless you're with people you know *very* well.

○ **Don't be a punster.** Most people hate puns. If you can't manage to hold back a pun, be prepared for groans! Then again, I often like to use puns while consciously anticipating the groans, as if to say, *I know, I know, isn't that horrible?*

How to Handle the Joker in Every Deck

As you know, there's usually one humor nitwit at every party. Besides escape, which is the subject of the next chapter, there are a couple of defensive techniques that will help. If it's a joke-telling joker, you can always say, "Oh yes, that's a funny one; I've heard it already," either to shut the joker up or to explain why you're not laughing. Or before the joker can get going, smile politely and say, "I'm afraid I'm just not really a joke person."

Let's say you are up against someone who seems to thrive on saying stupid things and then laughing at them. If you choose to stay in the vicinity of this person or for some reason cannot escape, you're going to have to decide whether to humor the idiot or try to squelch him. You can always try, "It's good to see you can crack yourself up like that." Or just smile vaguely until he gets the point that you don't think he's funny. In the end, we have to forgive even the worst jokers. They mean well, after all, and may simply be unsure of themselves, so always try to be kind.

On the other hand, if your tolerance is low and you are starting to feel like kicking and screaming, it may be time to . . . bail out and move on!

4 The Great Escape: Bailing Out and Moving On

When I speak of escaping, I do not mean leaving the social event itself. I'm talking about something much more difficult: how to remove yourself, as gracefully as possible, from a conversation. As almost everyone knows, getting into a conversation may be hard, but getting out is often much harder.

A friend of mine told me a story that positively made my skin crawl. He had attended a party—a business function—even though he had recently hurt his back and was in a fair amount of pain. Although he had gone to the affair with hopes of forgetting his troubles, his physical discomfort caused him to bring up the subject of his injury with a fellow guest. "You hurt your back?" the man said excitedly. "Boy, are you in for it now! You're going to have trouble with that now for the rest of your life! Let me tell you. . . ."

Realizing his mistake in introducing this literally painful topic, my friend tried weakly to change the subject, even going so far as to say that he really wasn't in the mood to talk about it, thank you. But the man would not stop.

". . . Believe me, I understand. What are you, about thirty? Well, it's all downhill from there. Listen to me, *all* my friends have chronic back pain. Whatever you do, don't have the surgery. You'll never be the same again, I'm telling you. . . ." Helplessly my friend tried to edge away, but the man had found his prey and went right along with him. It was a most unpleasant experience and went on for what seemed an eternity. My friend swore off parties for a month after that.

I have heard hundreds of similar stories, though most of them are not quite so terrible. Most of the time it is simply a question of being stuck in a conversation when you would rather be talking to someone else. The key to having a good time at parties is being able to choose whom you talk to and for how long.

Personally, I find that extricating myself from a person or small group takes more planning and effort than entering even the toughest of groups. In fact, it can be so difficult to get away from some people that many minglers just give up and settle in, resigned to the fact that they are probably going to be with this person for most of the evening. It often seems easier to stay put than to make the effort to move, especially if the current conversation isn't too dreadful. I even know one man who actually *tries* to get stuck; he seeks out another person at the party who shares his desire to stay in one place, with one person, the whole night, so that he won't have to worry about entering or exiting conversations.

Don't take the easy way out. The term "mingling" implies talking to a *lot* of people; if you remain in one place with no clue (or no inclination) as to how to move on, you're *not mingling*, no matter how great a conversation you are having. Naturally, if you discover the love of your life or the most fascinating person in the universe (or both, if you're lucky!), you may decide to stop moving around and stay where you are. That's OK, of course—but it isn't mingling! Mingling means circulating. And to circulate successfully, you have to know *when* to make your move and *how*.

WHEN TO MOVE

Boredom and Other Discomforts

The most obvious reason to move on is your own misery. Everyone has a personal tale of excruciating agony, that time they were hopelessly stuck with Mr. Obnoxious or Ms. Boring of the century. Usually a kind of inner panic sets in, and you try to talk yourself through it. ("OK, I'm going to get out of this. . . . Oh my God, this is terrible. . . . Why doesn't he just shut up for one second? . . . OK, I know I can get out of this somehow. . . .") while on the outside you smile with a glassy stare (the Glaze-out) and act as if you are listening. There's never any question about it in these cases. You need to get out as quickly, as permanently, and as gracefully as you can, whether you are imprisoned by a ditz, a drunk, a monologist, a wolf, a vamp, a joker, or just someone who wants you to get her a job. Remember, you can be selfish at a party. No guilt feelings are necessary; you are there to have fun. *You* decide what to drink, what to eat, and who to talk to and for how long!

Saving Face

The great thing about large parties is that if you do happen to make a faux pas, tell a joke that no one else thinks is funny, or otherwise embarrass or humiliate yourself, you can leave the witnesses behind and start over somewhere else with a fresh slate. Just forget your failure and try again with someone new.

The Case of the Vanishing Group

This phenomenon can be frightening to the minglephobic. Usually it begins without your even being aware of it; suddenly you notice there are fewer people in the group in which you have been engaged. The smaller the group gets, the harder it is going to be for you to get out. Also, in the Case of the Vanishing Group, there is usually a reason for its sudden shrinkage; namely, there's one person in the group who is a drag in some way. If you don't watch out, you're going to be the last one left, trapped with him or her, like the last rat on a sinking ship. Keep your eye out for the vanishing group, and leave before it's too late!

Time's Up!

Optimum mingling time is five to fifteen minutes per person or group (though there are some that last three minutes and some that may last thirty). You may be having a wonderful time, but you must move on. I know it's hard to leave when you're having fun, but remember: you are there to talk to as many people as you can. Tell yourself that you can come back to this person after you've met seven more people. Or get the person's card and ask him if you can get together one-on-one at another time. Take the good energy generated from the successful interaction and inject it into your next encounter!

Warning: Overzealous minglers may, however, move *too* quickly. I must plead guilty to doing this sometimes; I get so into the motion of mingling, the excitement of interaction, that I sometimes realize I am spending only thirty or forty seconds in one place. And that is definitely not enough time to do anything but leave a "Who was that masked man?" feeling behind.

THE ETIQUETTE OF ESCAPE

Knowing Where You're Headed

Before you employ any of the escape techniques described in this chapter, it's essential that you have a clear idea about where you are going next. Ideally, your next target will be a person or group, but you can also set your sights on a place (the bathroom, the bar, the food table, etc.). Many of the following escape lines include a mention of where you are headed, and of course you must at least pretend to do whatever you announce you are going off to do. If you decide you just want to walk around, be sure to plan your general route or direction in advance. For one thing, if there is any time other people may be watching you (which, as I pointed out in chapter 1, isn't likely), it's when you are leaving and entering cliques of people. Movement catches the eye, and if you break away from the group and are uncertain where to go next, you could end up looking lost and unwanted. The longer you are alone, not attached to any group, the more alienated you can feel, until you end up wondering why you left your last conversation anyway and how you can get back in. More important, if you don't appear to have a definite destination, the people you've just left could feel insulted, realizing that you would rather be alone than talk to them.

Always remember: The best time to scope out the room is when *you* are talking, especially if you are with only one or two other people. When someone is talking to *you*, you are required to maintain eye contact. However, if you are in a larger group, you can scan surreptitiously when you know the attention isn't focused on you. Try not to be caught looking off across the room, making it obvious you wish you were somewhere else.

The Five Laws of Survival

Mingling has its very own set of rules, many of which are different from the traditional standards of etiquette. Since it is during escape maneuvers that your sense of courtesy and graciousness will come in direct conflict with your instinct for survival, here are five laws to govern your exit behavior as a mingler, laws that you will find especially helpful to remember as you get ready to break away:

1. **It's OK to tell a lie.** That's right. Forget all that stuff you learned in school about George Washington and the cherry tree. George was probably terrible at parties. Lying for the purpose of mingling well is most assuredly in the white-lie category (see "The Philosophy of Fibbing: Why Lying Is Essential" p. 15) and it's the key to most exit techniques.

2. **No one knows what you are really thinking.** Even psychics can't read your exact thoughts. For the most part, other people know only what you *tell* them and what you *show* them.

3. **The other people are thinking primarily about themselves.** This is not just a mingling law but a life law. It helps to remember this one if you are nervous about people seeing through you or if you are overly worried about what people think about you.

4. **It's better to escape from someone than have someone escape from you.** Law 4 is a good motivator if you tend to procrastinate too much while preparing to escape; there's nothing more awkward at a party than being left standing by yourself.

5. **Change equals movement; movement equals change.** This is the most profound law and applies to all aspects of mingling

(as well as all aspects of life). The only real crime in mingling is stasis.

THE GETAWAY: TWELVE EXIT MANEUVERS

The Honest Approach in Reverse

When I talk about "honesty" in mingling, I'm not usually talking about truthfulness (which has nothing much to do with mingling) so much as a kind of *straightforwardness*. If you're like me and tend to be direct, you may want to use this exit technique whenever possible. It works only if you have been with one person or the same set of people for a respectable amount of time (ten minutes or so). As sincerely as possible, say something like: "Well, as enjoyable as this is, I think it's time for me to mingle," or, "Well, I don't want to monopolize your time, and anyway, I think we're supposed to mingle at this thing." Or you can use a version of one of the opening lines (p. 26): "Excuse me, but I really must go practice my mingling!" This maneuver constitutes a strong, definite form of exit; it announces your intention to leave in a manner that is not open to negotiation, and at the same time it offers an excuse that is more honest than many of the excuses people usually use to escape. It is, in fact, the most truthful line you can employ without admitting straight-out that you find the prospect of continued conversation with them unappealing.

Note: This exit technique works even better when it is coupled with the Honest Approach entrance. If your opening line has already established you as a guileless person and an enthusiastic mingler, people are going to buy this exit line much more readily.

The Fade-out

This one needs very little explanation; it is something that almost everyone who has ever attended a large party has done. It is appropriate for those times when you're not too involved in conversation—and hence you are not really trapped—and you simply want to move away as unobtrusively as possible.

As you may guess, the directions for the Fade-out are the exact opposite of those for the Fade-in technique (see p. 18). Wait until no one is talking to you or looking at you too closely and then . . . slowly start to back away. Watch and listen carefully as you begin your disappearing act, in case the conversation should happen to turn back to you in midfade. When you feel you are far enough away from the group to be unnoticed, make tracks!

Two warnings: You must not try this unless you are in a cluster of four (counting yourself) or more. Otherwise, you can be caught during Fade-out, and that can be extremely awkward. If you are caught—and this may happen, even while leaving a large group—you need to switch immediately into another escape tactic. So have one ready, just in case.

The Changing of the Guard

This well-known exit maneuver was one I had actually forgotten about until one night I attended a cocktail party on Manhattan's Upper East Side. I had set my mingling sights on a dashing-looking man I had met earlier during the party. He was standing in a group with two other people. I used the Fade-in (with just a smidge of the Touchy-Feely Mingle, something I'll talk about later), addressing my first remark to the man who was my primary target. The *second* I was "in," the other two guests took off, but fast! I was stunned by the sudden realization that my entrance had given them a way out and that this admittedly passive escape technique is used all the time, by practically everyone. I was so floored that my mouth fell open, and I just stood there like an idiot, staring at the disappearing duo. (Unfortunately, I was soon reminded of another truism, vis-à-vis the "dashing" man: Looks can be deceiving.)

This exit method works because of law 5: *Change equals movement; movement equals change.* As soon as a new person, or a new energy, enters the circle, a readjustment of some kind—no matter how subtle—automatically occurs. It's as though the new person has kicked up psychic dust, and while everyone is waiting for the dust to settle, people can slip away. I also call this strategy the Substitution Illusion, because the person exiting is using the illusion that because a new person is taking his place, it is now OK for him (the exiter) to leave. It's a fascinating aspect of mingling and makes for a totally facile escape. The drawback is obvious: To use the Changing of the Guard, you have to wait until someone new arrives. And it could be a very long wait.

The Smooth Escape

When you can pull this off, it makes you feel great—like a champion of minglers. It does, however, take a little finesse. What the Smooth Escape has going for it is that it works in drastic situations and, when done well, it's so subtle and natural that no one realizes they've just been handled.

The three steps of the Smooth Escape are: (1) take control of the conversation; (2) change the subject; and (3) exit gracefully. Easier said than done, I know. But here's an example.

Say you started out talking to a circle of four or five people, but one by one they have peeled off until you are left alone with Showy Joey, who has you pinned in a corner and is talking nonstop about his job as a computer salesman. Having failed to detect the Case of the Vanishing Group in time, you are now in one of the most challenging spots for any mingler. Don't despair. You *can* get out of this. But take a deep breath and concentrate, because you are going to need to be more alert for the Smooth Escape than you have been so far.

The first thing you must do is focus totally on what Joey is saying, so that you will be able to seize the slightest opportunity to wrest control of the dialogue. For example, as he is saying, ". . . so my real problem has been that in this economic climate most people are demanding a faster and faster system but aren't interested in paying for all the bells and whistles . . ." you can break in with, "By 'bells and whistles' do you mean things like DVD and CD burners?" *(You've taken control.)*

"Why . . . sort of. . . . I mean the drives are only . . . ," Joey might continue. Interrupt him again with something like, "Because my computer doesn't have any of that stuff. I don't even have a DVD player. I get so jealous when I am on the train and I see people watching movies on their laptops. Remember when people actually *talked* to each other on the train? But I still like the train better than taking a plane; don't you?" *(You've changed the subject.)* While Joey is busy trying to switch gears to follow you, keep talking: "And now, of course, trains are even *more* desirable because you don't have to go through all that security stuff, taking off your shoes and everything." At this point, while you are still speaking, focus on something across the room, as if something irresistible has caught your attention, touch Showy Joey's arm lightly, and say, "Excuse me a moment, won't you?" (And smile. It's always a good idea to be as warm as possible when you're leaving someone high and dry.) Then move quickly away.

The Smooth Escape can be a bit tricky, but keep the following in mind: If you act as if the conversation has been brought to its natural close and you've had a lovely time talking to Showy Joey, but the dance is over now, your behavior won't come off as rude. Don't forget, Joey has probably been run out on at parties most of his life. To him, it may be normal. The important thing to remember is that when you are really stuck with someone, the only way to get away is to take control of the situation.

Shake and Break

This escape route also involves taking control, but you have to have just the right circumstances to execute it properly. Use it only at a very large party, preferably a business party, when you are sure you are not going to mingle again with the same person or cluster. In other words, you have to be making your way through a large room of people, intending to leave when you have covered everyone, or you have to have a *very* good memory and avoid your Shake and Break victims for the rest of the night.

Suppose you are up against a talker like Showy Joey. As you are smiling at him and responding facially to what he is saying, stick your hand out until he instinctively takes hold of it, or just grab his hand (this won't work if he's got his hands in his pockets). Shake it until he either stops speaking or at least slows down; then smile warmly, and tell him, "It's been so nice meeting [talking with] you!" Then turn and walk away. In the opposite situation, where you are trapped with Mr. Awkward Silence, the Shake and Break technique is even easier, as you will not have to interrupt the flow of conversation. Just shake . . . and break!

The Human Sacrifice

Most people are too ashamed to admit that they use this device to escape from undesirable mingling partners, but I see it done at almost every gathering I attend. It's a clever maneuver because it poses as a social grace. The only prerequisite is that you know at least one other person at the party.

Imagine you are engaged in what seems an interminable discourse with Betsy the Bore. Before your mind numbs out completely, look around you and locate someone you either know or have just met. Proximity is important; you are going to have to be able to reach out and shanghai this third person. While nodding enthusiastically to what

Betsy is saying, pull this new person into your little twosome. Immediately you will feel a shift, a loosening of the bore's hold on you. Introduce the sacrificial lamb to the bore in a way that implies you are just being a good mingler by introducing two people who will probably have a lot in common. *As soon as their eyes meet,* leave. You must fade out of the conversation within thirty seconds or this conversational change of partners will not work. A pleasant "Excuse me" will also serve as an alternative to a Fade-out. As in ballroom dancing, you can't be considered rude since you have procured a new partner before moving on. But do remember the key here: *As soon as you have finished introducing the new person,* either do a fast fade or leave in a more overt manner, but get out quickly.

This trick works for the same reason the Changing of the Guard works: You've changed the cast of characters; you've brought in your own replacement. Of course, sophisticated minglers will know exactly what you're doing. In fact, I've been used as a sacrifice many times; I can spot the maneuver almost as soon as I'm summoned, but there's not much I can do except find another sacrifice as soon as I can or escape in some other manner. Obvious or not, the Human Sacrifice is still a perfectly acceptable move. All's fair in love and mingling!

Please keep in mind, however, that if you wait passively for a Human Sacrifice candidate to pass by, you could be stuck with Betsy the Bore till the end of time or the end of the party, whichever comes first. It's easiest if someone does pass right by you, of course, but there are many more active versions of this ploy. You can take the bore (if you're alone with her) by the arm and, while conversing, gently lead her across the room to another person or group. If she won't budge, you can interrupt her and say, "Do you mind if we join my friend over there?" Or even, "Betsy, let's go get some food [a drink]!" Once over by the food, where there will be a large cluster of people, you can lure a stranger into the conversation and then skedaddle, even if you have to use the bartender.

The Personal Manager

If you can't find a Human Sacrifice, you can try to motivate the person to leave *you*. This ploy requires a little acting skill and a lot of charm. Point out someone else in the room and say, "Oh look, there she is! . . . That woman over there is dying to meet you." Or, "I'm sworn to secrecy, but there's someone in that group there who is giving out free theater tickets [gift certificates/expensive cosmetics]." (Be sure to be vague about who this supposed philanthropist is.) Or wave in the general direction of a group and say, "I think you're being summoned." When your victim looks confused and asks, "By whom?" tell her, "I can't see him now, but he was waving to you . . . over there." There are countless ways of seducing the person into leaving you (you can tell her the food is disappearing fast or there's only one bottle of champagne left), and the great thing is, you can keep inventing until something works!

Escape by Mutual Consent

In all likelihood, this won't happen very often. When it does, it will result in great relief and maybe a slight amount of embarrassment.

Sometimes two people who end up talking to each other will realize at more or less the same moment that they are in a bad marriage, mingling-wise. They will simply look at each other and be able to tell that they both feel exactly the same way; either the dialogue between them is played out or they were mismatched in the first place. Usually one of them will smile sheepishly and say, "Well . . . ," and the other will respond, "Well, it's been nice to . . . ," and then the first one will say, "Good to talk to you!" And with a respectful nod or even a handshake, they'll turn away from each other at the same time and head off happily toward their next encounters. It's rare that such a clean and easy "divorce" occurs, but it does happen.

The Buffet Bye-Bye and Other Handy Excuses

Without question, this is the most commonly used escape technique, especially by men. (There are, in fact, some extremely fascinating mingling differences between the sexes.) What you do here is wait for any sort of lull in the conversation, then deliver one of the following excuses:

○ *"I've got to get some food."*

○ *"I am going to get something to drink."*

○ *"I must powder my nose"* (yes, I still sometimes use this euphemism, just for fun). Cutesy cat lover's version: *"I have to visit the sandbox."*

○ *"Excuse me, I have got to find my husband [wife/boy- or girlfriend/fiancé or fiancée]"*

○ *"Pardon me, but I simply must sit down!"*

○ *"I have to go outside for a cigarette."*

○ *"Do you have the time? . . . Really? I'm so sorry, I have to make a phone call."* (This excuse is commonly known as the Telephone Line.)

In spite of the ease with which these familiar excuses can roll off your tongue and their popularity among most partygoers, I myself do not use the Buffet Bye-Bye more than is absolutely necessary. When you use the "BBB," you must actually *do* what it is you have just announced you will do, even if you don't feel like it, and even if you are fairly sure your escape victim isn't looking. This can really cut into your party fun. Plus you can end up overeating, or drinking too much, or, worse still, *standing in line for the bathroom when you don't need to go!*

The other, very real danger with this technique is that the person from whom you are trying to escape may offer to go *with* you to the food table, the bar, the couch, outside for a smoke, or even to the bathroom. There is nothing for you to do in that case but agree cheerfully and hope you can shake the person off at the specified location. Also, depending on the situation and how old-fashioned you are, you may feel rude unless you offer to get the other person or even the whole group a drink, if you use thirst as your excuse. While it is, in general, acceptable to say you will return and fail to, *never, under any circumstances,* is it permissible to promise to fetch someone a drink and then not come back, though I know people who will deliver the proffered drink quickly and then move on. But it's not easy to do this smoothly.

My recommended choice of Buffet Bye-Bye excuses may surprise you: It's the Telephone Line. The reason is simple: Telephoning is a relatively private matter. Whether you are using the host's landline or your cell phone, no one (well, *hardly* anyone) will ever follow you. You must, of course, actually make a call. You can call the weather or the time, your own voice mail—or a friend to tell him to get his carcass over to the party.

Celling Out

In spite of the aforementioned efficacy of the Telephone Line, cell phones must be used sparingly at a party. Indeed, there are entire books written on cell phone etiquette; most people these days have a good sense of what crosses the line from practicality into bad manners.

Or so I thought until last Christmas. I was attending my cousin's building's holiday cocktail party, which I was gratified to discover featured excellent champagne, gourmet food, and elegant surroundings. I looked around, surveying the mingling arena, and—good grief! There, over by the food table, was an extremely well-dressed man who with one hand was dipping into the crudités and with the other was crudely cradling his cell. He was actually talking on the phone while he was grazing the buffet!

This is one of the worse cases of bad cell phone etiquette I have witnessed firsthand. Perhaps this man was merely oblivious to his surroundings and was in the middle of a business deal; however, it is also possible that, upon entering the party, he realized there was no one there he wanted to talk to and reached for his cell. In either case, if I had been the etiquette police I would have arrested him on the spot.

Used in moderation, however, cell phones and Blackberries do provide an excellent ruse for extricating yourself from hard-to-leave fellow guests. The conceit must be that your cell phone is on vibrate, as it is almost *never* good manners to have your cell phone on ring at a party (unless you are outside or the party is very loud and crowded—or you have a sick family member at home). Try to wait until a lull in the conversation, say, "Oops," or, "Shoot!" and go for your phone. Glance at it (the key to successful cell phone subterfuge is the look on your face; you must look aggravated at the interruption), shake your head apologetically, and move away from the group to a quiet corner or room to deal with your "important call" (or return the e-mail). Afterward you can rejoin the party—in another group of course, as if you were pulled there inextricably or just forgot where you had been.

Your cell phoniness can double as an exit from the party itself, should you find that you are desperate to leave before it is particularly polite to do so. If you do decide to leave the party, you can fabricate any number of believable—even intriguing—stories about whom you called and why you have to leave. Or you can just be cryptic and say, "I'm sorry, but I must leave right away," and dash out in a flurry.

The Counterfeit Search

Try this technique at your next party and I bet you will have enormous success with it. It requires a little body language, specifically use of the eyes.

It's especially easy to flow into this exit ploy if you have grown weary of the person who is talking to you. Your attention is probably already drifting, and you are going to be using any time you can to look around the room—either because you are scoping out your next conversational target or simply because you're bored. Try to follow the rule about scanning the room only while *you* are speaking; however, this is one time it may be necessary to let your eyes rove a bit while the other person is speaking to you. If you remember to look at the person intermittently you can get away with it. The trick is to give the impression that something inescapable is beginning to pull your attention away from your current conversational clique—totally against your will. To complete the maneuver, suddenly focus your eyes on someone (real or imagined) across the room and exclaim, "Oh!" Look embarrassed and confused for a moment, as if you didn't really mean to say that out loud. Then smile apologetically and say something like, "I'm so sorry, please don't think me rude, but there's a person over there I've been looking for since I arrived; he is supposed to have some freelance work for me," or, "Excuse me, will you, I just spotted someone I haven't seen for five years!" Or, at a business function: "Pardon me, but I just noticed a man across the room my boss particularly instructed me to talk to."

The Counterfeit Search can be a little abrupt, but if you put enough energy into making it look sincere, it's one of the quickest ways to exit. It is indubitably a bold maneuver, which is the very reason it works so well. People don't suspect this kind of lie; whereas every time anyone excuses himself or herself for a drink or something to eat, it smacks of escape. The other advantage to this technique is its quality of positive energy; you will appear to have so many people you need to talk to that you can't remain in one place—you're just dashing madly here and there! It can lend you an air of popularity. You may, of course, alter the line to make it comfortable for you. Some people prefer, "What the . . . ?!" (as in, "What the heck is *she* doing here!") to the more standard "Oh!" Use whatever comes most easily to you. Always leave your Counterfeit Search escape victims with the impression that you are going to come back to them as soon as you possibly can. So what if you never get around to it?

The Preemptive Strike: Dodgeball

Sometimes your advance warning system can allow you to escape before the fact. In certain rare emergencies, you might need to execute this preemptive escape technique:

You are having a quiet moment alone, sipping your martini and surveying the mingling field. Suddenly you notice a new arrival to the party. It's a woman you absolutely abhor. Every time you see her she insists on gossiping about other people who are present. To your dismay, she makes eye contact with you and you just know she is heading your way.

You've got to be quick on your feet to succeed at Dodgeball. As soon as you see this woman glance at you, you must not hesitate— not even for a microsecond. Don't smile at her; in fact, try to act as if you haven't seen her. You then make a beeline for a cluster of people who know you and who will let you into their protective custody, fast.

Of course the woman may very well suspect what you are up to, which is why Dodgeball should be used only when faced with the most torturous bores, bigots, or bad guys.

EMERGENCY ESCAPE HATCHES

If you really want to improve your mingling skills, I strongly suggest you learn and practice at least a few of the twelve exit maneuvers I have described. However, for use in a pinch, here are some quick and easy (some would say down and dirty) emergency escape lines:

- ○ *"Hold that thought. . . ."*

- ○ *"I'll be back. . . ."*

- ○ *"I'm sorry—I just remembered something. . . ."*

- ○ *"Got to go mingle!"*

- ○ *"Excuse me just a minute, won't you?"*

- ○ *"I'm not feeling well. . . ."*

- ○ *"I'm starving, excuse me. . . ."*

- ○ *"Excuse me, it's my contact lens. . . ."*

- ○ *"I think I just lost a filling. . . ."*

- ○ *"Oh my god—my wallet! It's gone!"*

5 Fancy Footwork: Advanced Mingling Techniques

Once you have some basic maneuvers down, you may want to try to expand your mingling repertoire and begin to fine-tune your mingling style. Remember: The more versatile and practiced you become as a mingler, the more enjoyment you will get from your social encounters, and the easier it will be to achieve whatever secondary goals you might have (getting a job, getting a promotion, getting a date, getting through another office Christmas party). And though most readers may not immediately be able to master every one of the following techniques and tricks, I think you'll find many of them familiar and some of them invaluable!

MINGLING STYLES FOR THE WELL SCHOOLED

The Quick-Change Artist

The more you come to understand the art of mingling, the more you will see the importance of being in control of your conversations. True mingling artists virtually shape each encounter using various tools of their trade, the most powerful one being the ability to change subjects easily. Most natural-born minglers have this Quick-Change talent without even realizing it, and unless they are mingling purely by entertaining, the Quick Change is probably their forte—the skill that makes them indestructible mingling machines.

To become a proficient Quick-Change Artist, you need to practice shifting your focus a bit during conversation, so that as you listen to the other person speak, you concentrate not only on your response to the person's comment or question but also on where you want the conversation to go next. I don't mean that you should not pay attention to the current conversation. The best minglers always at least *appear* to be fascinated by whatever is being said to them. But if you are on your toes, you can be ready to make a swift transition to a subject of your choosing before the people around you even know what hit them.

A good way to think about the process involved in the Quick Change is to imagine building a bridge. You and your conversational partners are currently on one side of the river; you want the group to be on the other side. The key is to find some material with which to build a bridge from one side to the other. If you simply interrupt and change the subject without making a connection between the old topic and the new one, you will usually come off sounding awkward or narcissistic. Remember: It can't look as if you have consciously manipulated the direction of the conversation; the dialogue must appear to flow naturally, as if it is taking its own course.

Let's say your conversational group is composed of a very interesting architect, the architect's husband, and another person. You would like to steer the conversation around to the architect, as you have seen her buildings and admired them. At present, however, the architect's husband is going on at length about his garden, which you find about as interesting as cardboard. Everyone else is standing there, passively listening, or making innocuous comments such as, "Oh, I've seen those; they're beautiful," or, "Do those bloom all year round?" As a Quick-Change Artist, you can decide exactly where you want to be, conversationally, and it should take you no time at all to get there. Imagine all the possible connections between the two subjects, select one, and then head for the bridge.

For instance, you can turn to the architect and say something like, "Planning houses in a community is like planting a garden in a way, isn't it?" Or, "Do you work closely with the landscapers on the gardens and lawns for your buildings?" The architect will answer, and you will be able to continue in your chosen course of conversation, taking pride in the fact that you have succeeded in creating a more interesting environment not only for yourself but also (probably) for at least two of the other three people in your clique.

Admittedly, some subjects are harder to move away from than others. And there are some people who are adamantly determined to talk about whatever it is they are determined to talk about. If you really get good at changing subjects, however, you can outmaneuver anyone and/or escape if necessary.

Another way to approach the Quick Change is to use free association. This method can really keep the ball in your court, which is where you want it, because it's always an advantage if *you* get to serve. For example, if someone is chattering away about flowers, take the word "flower" and let it lead you to another word, the first word that pops into your mind. In other words, think, *Flower—bee.* Then you ask, as if it is really puzzling you, whether bees pollinate all flowers or just some. When the floral expert answers, you can then safely complete the subject switch by remarking that you have an uncommon fear of bees, or that you are allergic to bees, or did everyone know that after bees sting you they die, and isn't that true justice? This last remark can lead to a discussion of aggression and justice, which can end up being a whole lot more interesting than flowers and fertilizer.

Free association is used often by the Quick-Change Artist, for two reasons. First, it's more flexible and open-ended than bridge building. That is, you aren't necessarily trying to get from point A to point B; you are simply moving away from point A, either because A is boring or distasteful to you or because you want to be in control of the dialogue. The other reason free association works so well for the Quick-Change Artist is that the subject you move to is probably right on the tip of everyone else's brain also. The change will usually seem perfectly natural and not at all forced. A good Quick-Change Artist can, in this manner, lead the conversation of a whole group rapidly and elegantly from one topic to another, so that everyone—including the Artist herself—has a good time.

The Pole-Vaulter

A more extreme form of subject changing is called Pole-Vaulting. A Pole-Vaulter is someone who is a facile topic jumper and a master of the non sequitur. People who can change subjects drastically and in the blink of an eye—without coming off as either demented or terribly rude—command amazing power in all their interactions. If you can Pole-Vault well, you can actually leap right over to where you want to be.

Given the aforementioned garden conversation, a fairly pedestrian Pole-Vault subject change might be something like: "There are so many different kinds of flowers . . . I can never tell one from the other; I'm handicapped that way! . . . But hey, before I forget to ask, how old do you think this apartment building is?" Or, "Well, I don't know about that, but I do know that I'm starving at the moment." In both of those cases, there is a short kind of wrap-up before the actual Vault. More abrupt, without the wrap-up, would be a sudden interjection like, "Have you heard that Hillary Clinton is getting a divorce?" which even if it isn't true is intriguing enough to lead someone off the track.

Some subject changes are more aggressive than others. If you sense someone is about to bring up the touchy subject of your soon-to-be ex-wife in front of your girlfriend, you might interrupt him with an alarming non sequitur like, "Excuse me, but is that a mole? On your cheek there? You'd better get that checked out; that doesn't look too good." Other generic non sequiturs include: "I'm sorry—I just this second remembered a strange dream I had last night," and "Wait . . . I'm having déjà vu."

Warning: Do not use the Pole-Vaulter when you haven't been listening. (It is *not* intended as a substitute for the Dot-Dot-Dot Plot.) It is important that no one is in the middle of a conversation about the death of her dog or upcoming cancer surgery when you start vaulting. You could end up flat on your face.

The Playful Plagiarist

Have you ever been in a wedding reception line where you had to talk to hundreds of people, one right after the next? You probably had absolutely no idea what to say to any of them and your face started to hurt from trying to smile so much. It was while in such a desperate situation that I—happily—stumbled upon the Playful Plagiarist style of mingling. It's perfect for reception lines, award ceremonies, and other occasions where you are the center of attention (your coming-out party, your art opening, your fiftieth birthday) and people are coming at you, fast and furious.

Let's say you are the maid of honor at a wedding. As if it weren't bad enough that you have to stand there in a horrible pink polyester chiffon maid-of-honor getup, you are being forced to stand in your dyed-to-match, uncomfortable pumps and shake hands with an unending stream of guests, most of whom you don't know and couldn't care less if you ever saw again. You have only a couple of minutes to speak with each person, and because all you really want is for reception-line duty to be over so you can have a drink or something to eat, your natural tendency is to take a totally passive stance, that is, to smile as nicely as possible and say "thank you" to the obligatory comment that you certainly do look beautiful.

This is, of course, perfectly acceptable social behavior. But if you consider the fact that the guests moving through the line are just as bored as you are at having to take part in this outmoded reception-line ritual, why not try to make it fun? Having fun is, after all, your objective in every mingling situation. And believe me, if you can make interesting conversation in a wedding reception line, the word is going to get around that you are a social success. Here's what you do.

Take something someone says to you and use it on the next person who approaches you, as if it is your own idea. For example, if Mrs. Smithers says to you in parting, "How nice it is that the bride and groom found each other after all these years," when Mr. Johnson greets you next you can ask him if *he* doesn't think it's wonderful that the bride and groom have found each other after all these years. Then when Mr. Johnson says, "Yes, they make a lovely couple," you can say to the next person, "Don't Joe and Sally make a lovely couple?" And when that person says, oh yes, she's never seen such a beautiful bride, the next thing on your lips can be a remark about how the bride is the loveliest bride you've ever seen.

By using the Playful Plagiarist, you can avoid using one line over and over and at the same time you don't have to think up new things to say at 60 miles per hour. Although the examples I have given might not be too hard to think up yourself, in tiring mingling situations it's much more relaxing if you let others do some of the work. A little conversational petty theft, and people will get the impression you have a natural social sense. In fact, it will appear as if you are never at a loss for words.

The Playful Plagiarist technique can be useful in "normal" party circumstances also, though it may call for a little more panache in its execution. At a typical large party, using this style requires taking a line or comment you hear in one group with you and delivering it when you are safely inside another group (sometimes you can even use it as an entrance line). For example, if someone remarks that this is the tenth party your host has had in one year, the next time you are in another group of people and in need of something to say, you can repeat the line, especially as it is a general party observation and will fit in at just about any pause.

Warning: Occasionally, someone may *recognize* your stolen line as having come from someone other than you, either because there's a witness from the first group present or because the comment has un- mistakable characteristics. If you think there's any possibility of get- ting caught with your hand in the till, the best thing to do is give authorship: Start or follow the line with, "So-and-so was saying that . . ." That way no one will think of you as an unoriginal sap who is reduced to stealing bits of conversation—yet you still get to use the material!

Trivial Pursuits

Some people have a gift for remembering bits of trivia; others (like me) don't. There's no way that I know of to change a non-trivia- minded person into one of those human fact magnets we all know and love. However, if you *are* an automatic storer of trivia, you have a great asset to your mingling style, as long as you keep in mind the following:

1. **If you've got it, flaunt it.** If you do have interesting tidbits of information at your fingertips, by all means share them. Trivia and mingling are close cousins—they're both light, interesting,

nonthreatening human interaction. But keep it within reason, please. No one enjoys talking to people who spew trivia every time they open their mouths.

2. **Wait for an appropriate place in the discussion.** This is absolutely essential in playing the mingling game of Trivial Pursuits. Your fun fact must be relevant to the conversation and be offered up in just the right place, so it doesn't seem forced, or as if you are showing off your trivia prowess. For example, if you suddenly want to bring up the fact that the word for having a fear of getting peanut butter stuck to the roof of your mouth is "arachibutyrophobia," there'd better be some peanut butter being consumed.

3. **Don't maneuver the conversation for the sole purpose of delivering a piece of trivia.** This is taboo, even though good minglers have the skill to do it. If the item you have is so earth-shatteringly fascinating that you feel compelled to offer it, just jump in and do it, if you must. But don't spend time and energy manipulating the discussion so that your piece of trivia will fit in. You may get caught at it, and that can be *very* embarrassing. In fact, to put it bluntly, you could end up looking like a trivia nerd. Trivia buffs are considered entertaining only if they are not too obsessed with their trivia.

4. **Make sure of your audience.** Watch carefully when you deliver your first trivial fact. Do the others in the group seem interested? Sometimes people find certain trivia to be an intrusion in the flow of dialogue or even boring. There's no way to tell whether or not you use trivia well except to study the reactions of those around you. Do eyes roll or glance away? Do you hear a lot of throat clearing? Make sure you're not being obnoxious.

The Art of Piggybacking

Piggybacking is a very familiar concept in mingling, and I know many people who swear by it as a mingling style. It's not exactly the most *courageous* tack to take, but it can be used continually, from your first opening line up until the time you leave the party.

Many minglers use this technique without thinking about it, it's so simple. It entails merely attaching yourself briefly to another person to get from one place to another.

Imagine that you arrive at a party where just about the only person you know is the hostess. No problem. Just latch on to that hostess and hang on for dear life (figuratively speaking, that is; you are *not* encouraged to actually hold on to coattails or skirts during this maneuver!) until such time as she leads you over to someone else and introduces you—or until someone new joins you and the hostess. Have no fear, for one of these two things will happen within minutes, if she's any kind of hostess at all. Now you have a new acquaintance to tag along with, and you can follow this person into another group, where you can find new people to trail. In this way you can leapfrog from conversation to conversation, always appearing to have many friends and never at a loss for a conversational companion. Even if, for some reason, the hostess *doesn't* hook you up with another guest but just gestures to the far end of the room and says, "Feel free to help yourself at the bar," you can still employ the Piggyback technique—after you've introduced yourself to one or two people using other methods first.

The real art of Piggybacking lies in the way you follow people. Like a good gumshoe tailing someone, pretend you don't notice when your Piggybacking target leaves the circle of people; wait a few seconds, and then casually follow in his wake. Remember the Changing of the Guard escape technique? It's very easy to move off right after someone else has exited, if you do it quickly enough. The idea is to make your target think, when he sees you've followed him into a new group, that it's only a coincidence or that you found his conversation interesting enough to want more of it. Never let him know that you are using him to help you move in and out of groups; get caught doing the Piggyback and people will think you are a real baby.

Please note: It's essential that you remember to switch Piggyback targets as often as possible. It's against the basic precepts of mingling to stay with one person for any substantial length of time. Never forget my earlier maxim: *He who mingles best mingles alone.* (Of course I never said you couldn't occasionally have a little help.)

The Butterfly Flit
(EXPERTS ONLY)

Picture a country meadow on a summer day. In fact, if you can, go *visit* a country meadow on a summer day. Watch how the butterfly dances lightly upon the flowers. Notice how quickly and gently it touches each one—barely brushing like a whisper over some while resting gracefully for long moments on others. The butterfly flies free; each flower it visits is honored by the butterfly's brief stay, and each perfumed encounter becomes forever a part of its fluttering experience.

Pardon me for waxing poetic, but this is the image you must hold in your mind while attempting the challenging Butterfly Flit. It is with this technique that mingling becomes an art form, and like any true art, it is hard to describe in concrete terms or by using step-by-step directions.

The Butterfly Flit can encompass any or all of the techniques, lines, and tricks in this book. Your objective is to, using all the mingling knowledge and instinct at your disposal, weave your way through the clusters of people, stopping for thirty seconds or so at each to check them out. If you decide a group is interesting or challenging enough for you to make a mingling commitment, you enter the group more fully and remain for a five- or six-minute period. Then you're off again, leaving your ex-group breathless, wishing you had stayed longer and hoping you'll return soon.

Just exactly how, choreographically, you manage the Butterfly Flit without looking as if you have ADD or without being impolite to anyone or knocking anything over is too complicated to describe. If you are ever feeling truly inspired or socially brilliant, go ahead and give the Flit a whirl. It's one of those things you can learn only by doing. But, frankly, I do not recommend it for most minglers.

GIMMICKS FOR THE CONFIDENT MINGLER

When the circumstances are right and you are feeling game, the following gimmicks can add spice to your evening and variety to your mingling experience. Unlike the mingling styles I have just described, however, mingling gimmicks are for occasional use only. Your limit per party should be one or two times for each trick.

A Case of Mistaken Identity

I know you've probably seen countless versions of this ploy in bad B movies. Historically it has been used as a pickup line, which is why I try never to use it except when my motives are purely conversational. You guessed it; it's the old "Pardon me, I thought you were someone else!" This is such a cliché that it actually works, probably because most people can't believe that anyone would try this line if it weren't true.

There are many enjoyable and effective ways to carry off this daring opening maneuver. The easiest and safest is to come up behind your "mark" and confidently touch or tap him or her on the shoulder. Your big "I'm so glad to see you" smile should fade by the time the

person finishes turning around and be replaced by a confused, surprised look. Then you can say something like, "I'm so sorry . . . from
the back, I swear, you look just like someone else [my old roommate/
my neighbor]." I sometimes even like to add, "God, that sounds like
a line, doesn't it?" In any case, by this time you've more or less entered the group and you can go ahead and follow your Mistaken
Identity entrée with any number of conversational moves, including
just plain introducing yourself.

There are, as you can imagine, more outrageous ways to use a Case
of Mistaken Identity, all of which can make a lasting impression but
can also get you into trouble. You can pinch the person, tap him on
the head, slap him smartly on the back, even kiss him on the neck. All
of these things imply an intimacy that must be equaled by your embarrassment when you discover your "mistake." The drawback with
these more extreme versions: Often the victim is so offended and the
other people in the group so startled that the thought of actually joining them becomes distasteful to you.

Always remember, however, that should this gimmick backfire and
you find yourself greeted with hostility or any other unwelcoming
behavior, the very nature of the lie will allow you to withdraw without losing face. After all, it wasn't the person you were looking for,
right? You didn't mean to approach this group anyway; it was all a
mistake. With a parting apology, you're out of the group, free and
clear, ready to try it again (on someone on the other side of the room,
please) or to put away the gimmick for another day.

Fumbling In

A lot of these techniques may seem a bit crude, but advanced mingling
doesn't mean subtlety; it only means that the methods require more skill
or finesse. So while Fumbling In may seem like a rough-and-tumble

way of entering a conversation, it actually takes an accomplished mingler to perform it correctly.

The perfect model for this gimmick is Peter Falk in *Columbo*. His
character, who seems on the surface to be a bumbling idiot, is really
a brilliant tactician who can disarm people with his clumsy act. It is
with Columbo's particular form of graceless artfulness (or artful
gracelessness) that you are going to approach this opening gambit.

Select your target group. Edge toward them, making certain no
member of the group is looking at you. With your back or at least
your side to them, pretend to be concentrating hard on something
across the room, and then . . . "accidentally" bump into someone in
the group. Not too hard; for this particular trick, you don't want to
cause drink spillage or personal injury, just jostle them enough for at
least one person to notice and acknowledge your presence. After you
say you're *terribly* sorry (this has to be convincing), usually it is easy to
join their conversation. If, however, you should be confronted with
any hostility, like, "Hey, Why'nt ja look where you're going!" have
some believable explanation ready. "Someone pushed me," is always
good, though I also like the more self-denigrating, "I *am* sorry, really, I
don't know what is the matter with me—been a clumsy oaf all day!"
With the latter excuse you still have a chance that your fumble will
succeed; your taking responsibility for your klutziness may endear you
to some of the group and alleviate some of their initial bad humor.

The real beauty of Fumbling In is that if the gimmick does fail
and you are ignored or rebuffed or if you decide that you made a bad
selection and you don't want to stay in the group after all, it's the easiest thing in the world for you to move on. You can't be rejected, because you didn't ask to join their group; it was an accident! In effect,
nothing has been ventured, and therefore nothing is lost.

Note: Fumbling In should be attempted only in a fairly crowded
room. If there are miles of space between people, you're just going to

look foolish or, worse, drunk. It's bad enough if you do get drunk at a party, but it's an absolute crime to *appear* drunk.

The Interruption Eruption
(EXPERTS ONLY)

Please pay attention to the Experts Only label on this one. Even I rarely attempt this stunt, though it's a heck of a lot of fun when it succeeds. You have to be feeling absolutely fearless.

Let's assume you *are* an expert mingler, with years of experience under your belt. You are at a fun party and are feeling adventuresome. You have just ducked smoothly out of a conversation you had grown weary of and are scanning the room for a new set of mingling partners. Suddenly you spot it: a laughing, glittering cluster of four or five people over by the cake. They look like a tight group, an invigorating challenge for you to try to enter. You quickly run through the many entrance maneuvers in your mind and decide on . . . the Interruption Eruption. When you feel quite ready, you take a deep breath, move boldly up to the group, push your way firmly in between two people—without waiting for them to stop talking—and say, loudly and with great energy, "Hello there! How are you all? Hey, I don't think I've met a single one of you yet! My name is . . ."

It's not so much what you say in the Interruption Eruption as how you say it. Your demeanor must communicate that you are so certain of your charms that you know that everyone will be happy that you've come to talk to them, even though you have more or less exploded, uninvited, into their conversation. As you may suspect, there is a dangerously thin line between this technique and rudeness, so the important thing is to exude *extreme* warmth to everyone in the group after you are in. You must positively *beam* goodwill at everyone, and at the same time you must lead the conversation for a while. People will expect you to perform after such an entrance.

You can use almost any line for the Interruption Eruption; you can even use a question, such as one of the game-playing questions on page 48 ("Excuse me! What color would you say this [——] is?") A question is usually a bit more abrasive here, but if it is a very good question, one that someone will snap up right away, it can be a quicker way in. The best kind of question to use is one that indicates an ongoing debate or poll taking, such as, "Hey, what have you guys heard about the Smith Company warehouse burning down?" Not only will your eagerness for information help excuse your interruption, but also people tend to forget that you've barged in on them when there's an interesting query before them.

The Interruption Eruption is a strong, daring mingling gimmick, which can be positively thrilling when you are victorious. However, if it doesn't work, you are in serious, serious trouble. One time I interrupted a group with a brazen, "Hi, guys! Gosh, isn't it hot in here?" Well, you might have thought I'd just shot someone. Everyone looked at me with a mixture of distaste and astonishment, and one man said, "Excuse me, whoever you are . . . we were in the middle of a conversation!" Upon which I slunk away, tail between my legs. But of course I recovered. And so will you.

The Quotation Device

Many of my acquaintances swear by the Quotation Device. For some sticky situations—and especially in certain circles—this particular gimmick can be just the thing to create a sense of camaraderie between strangers. If you have any sense of the dramatic at all, you will discover that if you aren't using this one already, you should be.

Here's how it works: When someone says something that makes you or anyone else feel uncomfortable, or when you are at a loss for something to say, or just if it seems like the perfect moment, just pop in one of the following famous quotes from movies or TV shows. Your listeners will love it; it relaxes most people immediately. Whether or not we like to admit it, television and film are more of a common denominator than race, religion, financial status, or occupation. What you are actually doing with the Quotation Device is relieving psychological tension by calling forth a common cultural image. It almost always lightens the atmosphere, and it has the added benefit of being the kind of conversational punctuation mark that can allow you to change the subject or even exit from the group. Two rules: The line must be familiar to people (different media work in different crowds—for example, if you are at an event in Manhattan, *Seinfeld* lines are a sure thing), and you must quote it correctly.

Note: You are *not* to cite the source of the quote unless prompted. (Anyway, it's usually a bad sign if they have to ask!)

Here are some of my favorites:

LINE	USE
"I think this is the beginning of a beautiful friendship." (Casablanca)	When flattered, for general amity, or right before you hand someone your business card
"Frankly, my dear, I don't give a damn!" (Gone with the Wind)	When insulted or when dealing with a vicious gossip
"Years from now, when you talk of this—and you will—be kind." (Tea and Sympathy)	After a faux pas, like right after you have asked a nonpregnant woman when she is due
"Fasten your seat belts. It's going to be a bumpy night." (All About Eve)	After having witnessed an argument or an insult or upon seeing the host's uninvited ex-wife arrive

LINE	USE
"That's a horse of a different color." (The Wizard of Oz)	When stalling for time or after having been asked something you can't or won't answer
"It is a far, far better thing I do than I have ever done." (A Tale of Two Cities)	Upon setting off to get someone a drink, after having been asked to do any favor, or when heading toward a long bathroom line
"Not that there's anything wrong with that!" (Seinfeld)	After a politically incorrect comment, especially about someone being gay
"No soup for you!" (Seinfeld)	At the buffet table, upon realizing the food is gone
"These pretzels are making me thirsty!" (Seinfeld)	When eating pretzels
"Lu-cy . . . you've got some s'plainin' to do!" (I Love Lucy)	After drink spillage, messy food dropping, or the staining of furniture
"Shall we go for the 'Full Monty'?" (The Full Monty)	When going for seconds at the buffet table
"Beam me up, Scotty." (Star Trek)	When you've just knocked over a lamp or revealed to Bob's girlfriend that you used to date Bob
"You're entering another dimension . . ." (The Twilight Zone)	Upon a shift in the party atmosphere: a drastic music change, the arrival of a large group, or when someone brings out a case of tequila

Making the Most of Toasts

Most people make toasts only at weddings or awards dinners. Toast making at a sit-down dinner is a pretty straightforward proposition, but contrary to what you may think, a toast can be made anywhere, anytime—even while mingling.

"Anytime" is a slight exaggeration. You do have to have a glass in your hand to make a toast. But given that small requirement, you can throw one in at practically any time, for various effects. For instance, you can recover from a faux pas ("A toast! To carpet cleaners!"), soothe an argument ("Here's to a difference of opinion!"), field an insult ("To charm—something you might like to learn more about sometime!"), or even exit from a group ("To [whatever is being discussed] everywhere! Excuse me.").

You can throw in a toast in the more obvious situations, of course, such as after someone has just brought you a drink ("Here's looking at you—thanks!") or after somebody makes an announcement ("To Joe's new job; the best of luck!"). You could also use toasts to change the subject, specifically to take the heat off yourself, if someone is asking you questions you'd rather not answer or is making you uncomfortable with too much attention. Simply pick out someone else in your group and make a toast to her, or take the too-personal subject and make a toast to the subject in general.

Usually you will want to wait for a pause before proposing your toast. But often if you simply raise your glass while someone is still talking, the speaker will pause—sometimes in midsentence—and you can make your toast. All of us are trained to stop whatever it is we are doing and pay close attention when someone raises a glass. Never forget that toasts are very powerful social weapons and that they can be an important part of your conversational arsenal.

Two toast tips: (1) Never down the entire contents of your glass after a toast, unless you have only a small amount left or unless you are in a place (Russia, for example) where this might be considered the norm. (2) If your glass is empty when someone proposes a toast, just raise the empty glass in tribute. *Don't* pretend to drink, and *don't* say, "Hold that toast until I get something in my glass." (Unless it is a partywide toast; in that case there will be a designated glass filler nearby.)

SOPHISTICATED BODY BUSINESS

Not all conversing is done with the mouth. Your whole body speaks every time you move. Body language is important to learn for all areas of life, but for the would-be mingling expert there are three particular pieces of body "business" you may want to study.

The Mysterious Mingle

The Mysterious Mingle is really about poise. So far in this book I have been telling you what you can say, when you should say it, and how you should say it. But there are times in mingling when the best line to use is no line at all.

To carry off this technique, you must project the attitude that you have a great many fascinating things to say, but that *tonight* you'd rather listen to others and kind of soak up life. Some Mysterious Minglers prefer to put a little ho-hum feeling into their presentation; others lean more toward the intriguing "I've got a secret" look. In either case, your posture must be erect but nonchalant and your facial expression should be attentive, pleasant, and, above all, confident. It may help you to employ the Pros and Icons survival fantasy (p. 5), at least for the first time you try this.

As you move through the room, keep your arms and legs relaxed, and don't hurry anywhere. The world is your oyster. Life is a bowl of cherries (and any other platitude of this nature you can think of). You are going to listen contentedly to conversation and answer thoughtfully when called upon, but never with more than a few words. Use an enigmatic smile whenever you can (practice this—it has to *look* enigmatic, not just feel it). Whether you are quietly entering a group (this is the only time you're allowed to use the Fade-in without completing the maneuver by saying something), exiting a group, or just standing by yourself somewhere, remember: You are not at a loss for words; you've just put them away . . . for now. By choice. Your body stance, your eyes, mouth, eyebrows—every part of you—have got to say, *I like people very much, but I really don't care at all what they think of me.*

There's something very powerful about a person who does not talk when everyone else is working so hard at conversation. If you do the Mysterious Mingle well, people will be so interested in trying to find out what your story is and why you're not talking about it that you could find yourself becoming—silently—the center of attention.

Note: It's not a good idea to try to get away with a Mysterious Mingle pose when you suddenly find you can't think of anything to say. People will sense the difference, unless you are an extremely good actor. There are, after all, other, much easier things to do when you draw a blank. Also, be sure you are coming off as mysterious and not supercilious. You don't want people to think you just can't be bothered talking to the likes of them.

The Touchy-Feely Mingle

Never underestimate the power of human touch. A small amount of the right kind of touching while you are mingling can add a comforting sense of warm intimacy to your conversations. The wrong kind of touching, however, or too much touching can be one of the most serious faux pas you can make without taking off all your clothes on the ballroom floor.

When employing the Touchy-Feely Mingle, always err on the side of not enough rather than too much. If you have to, tell yourself you have only so many touches to give out for the whole night, so you have to use them sparingly.

Use the Touchy-Feely only when you are involved in a fairly absorbing conversation with one other person. It doesn't have to be a tête-à-tête—there can be others standing with you in the group—but you and this other person should be doing most of the talking. Watch the other person's face carefully to see if he or she is truly engaged in the discussion. At an appropriate place during a time when *you* are speaking (the punch line of a joke, the climax of a story, the main point in a discussion, or when you are getting ready to end the conversation), lean forward slightly and clasp or touch the person's forearm or upper arm briefly, then let go. It should be not *quite* a squeeze yet more than just a brush. Now—and this is important—regard the person carefully during this touch, watching in particular the eyes. You should be able to tell if your touch has enhanced the exchange or hindered it. Unless you are certain that the effect was a positive one, *do not touch this person again.*

Other types of Touchy-Feely mingling include resting your hand briefly on the shoulder of someone standing next to you, touching someone lightly on the back (not the small of the back, please; that's a little *too* intimate for mingling), taking someone's elbow as you move across the room together. For the most part, any other kind of touching during mingling is unacceptable. The Touchy-Feely Mingle, when done with sensitivity, can make a five-minute conversation a warmer, more enjoyable experience. But remember, a little goes a long way. There's nothing quite so unpleasant as being repeatedly pawed by some thick-skulled lout.

The Beauty of Bowing

Bowing is an excellent nonverbal device—elegant, humorous, and effective—for both men *and* women. The beauty of bowing is three-fold: Hardly anyone does it anymore, it is unusual, and it can communicate many things. In fact, it is amazing how many different meanings can be conveyed with different kinds of bows. I recommend trying at least one of the following bows, if only to see how much fun and how versatile bowing can be:

THE BOW	THE MEANING
The Hi Bow: A friendly, small bow. Leaning forward slightly from the waist, you retain eye contact and offer a sincere smile.	*Greetings. I'm happy to have you join us.*
The Ah, Yes Bow: A medium to small bow of either just the head or the whole upper body, eyes closed during bow, smile optional.	*I agree.*
The Touché: A very slight incli-nation of the head and neck, along with a slow closing of the eyes and just the hint of a wry smile.	*You got me!*
The Grateful Bow: A fairly deep bow of the head, done with one or two hands on the chest and a broad but closed-mouth smile.	*Thank you kindly for the compliment, sir or madam.*

THE BOW	THE MEANING
The Humble Bow: With hands clasped in front of you as if in prayer, a bow of the head, neck, and shoulders. Close eyes briefly while bowing.	*I defer to your greater wisdom in the matter.*
The Punctuation Mark: A full, dramatic bow from the waist, one hand on the stomach and the other hand on the back. The head turns slightly to the side. Stay in bowed position for one or two seconds before coming back to an upright position.	*My story is over. Thank you for listening.*
The Curtain Bow: Deep, full-bodied bow, arms dramatically outstretched, eyes open or closed; turn away as you come back up	*Good-bye, it's been an honor to talk to you.*
The Sarcastic Bow: Click your heels together sharply, stand up stiffly at attention, then bow fully and quickly in mock military fashion. No smile.	*You're such a fascist, I'm not even going to honor that remark with a response.*

CONVERSATION PIECES: USING PROPS

Jewelry and Accessories

Whether it's a feather hat or a pin that says: "Clone me," wearing an unusual accessory almost guarantees that you'll never have to endure the trauma of the Awkward Silence. Invariably, the first (or second) thing people will say to you is, "Wow, what a wonderful [odd, awful, unique, colorful] pin that is!" Not only does this prop provide them with easy subject matter—for which any minglephobic is always grateful—but it also causes them to introduce a topic for which you're totally prepared. You are now on home turf, because it's your accessory, after all, and you have probably already had many conversations about it. You have stored up a wealth of material from which to choose (for example, where you got the particular pin, about wearing pins in general, the origin of pin wearing, etc.), and you've already rehearsed your lines.

The best conversation pieces by far are earrings, hats, and eyeglasses. These work best because they are worn on the head. The next best are pins, necklaces, scarves, and ties. Once you get below the waist—with shoes, stockings, pants—you are in more personal territory; things that are attached to the lower part of the body enter the area of personal attire. And most people will at least hesitate before commenting on your clothing—unless someone has on such an extraordinarily striking outfit that it would be almost rude *not* to comment.

Below is a list of accessories, in order of effectiveness, that can assist you in your mingling experience. Pick an accessory that is particularly beautiful, funny, cool, unusual, thought-provoking—or handmade by you. *Note:* If it's got a symbol on it, be sure you know what it is you're saying!

○ *earring(s)*

○ *eyeglasses*

○ *pin or button*

○ *handbag*

○ *necklace, watch, bracelet, or ring*

○ *tie, scarf, or shawl*

○ *gloves*

○ *a fan (fans would be too theatrical in some circles but not in the South; on a hot day, why not?)*

Gadgets and Other Paraphernalia

Before smoking became practically a felony, I was a dedicated cigarette smoker. I also had *the* coolest, most extraordinary, most beautiful cigarette case anyone had ever seen. It was made of sleek blue and white Art Deco plastic and contained fourteen separate cylindrical compartments that held one cigarette each. It had springs, so that when you bent it in two you could expose exactly one cigarette. Whenever I took out this case, people would ooh and aah and ask to examine it. It was a superb mingling prop. But I never knew just what a treasure I had until one fateful night in Chicago.

My friend Cathy and I had decided to check out a bar we had heard was "fun." We weren't familiar with the neighborhood, and when we got there I knew why. The cab left us before we had a chance to turn back. "Oh well," we said to each other, "how bad could it be?" We certainly weren't going to be chicken.

P.S. We should have been chicken. A big hairy guy with rings in his nose let us in. A smirk on his face plainly said, *These little girls don't know what they've just gotten themselves into.* We looked around nervously. This was in the early eighties, when punk bars were really punk—violent, scary places with chains and knives and danger—not the pseudopunk clubs of later on. Cathy and I didn't know much about punk bars then. But we were about to find out.

Everyone stopped talking when we came in. (I might mention that we were wearing fifties-style swing skirts and sweaters with sweet little pearl buttons.) All we could see was big hairy tattoos with arms attached and dark, scabby faces staring intensely at us. Gulping, we stepped gingerly up to the bar and tried to act as though we were not in terrible trouble. The bartender, a huge man with a couple of safety pins through his cheek, leaned toward us and glared.

"Uh . . . um . . . ," I managed to say, "a martini, please?"

Cathy smiled a brave smile. "And a Miller Lite?"

Silence. Nobody moved. Panic was closing in; I could feel Cathy tensing. Any minute we were going to have to get up and run, but run where?

I decided I really needed a cigarette. That's when it happened. As soon as the bartender spotted my cigarette case, he growled, "Lemme see that thing." Shaking, I handed it to him. He studied it, opened it, and then . . . he smiled.

In that split second, the entire bar relaxed. Our bartender, who turned out to be a rather decent fellow named Chris, showed the case to everyone in the place, and we were immediately accepted. The cigarette case had, miraculously, been our ticket in. This mingling prop saved the day; in fact, we ended up having a surprisingly good time.

I'm not saying that your prop will keep you from being killed as mine did for us, but there is no question that a prop can give you something to do as well as something to talk about. In fact, I don't think there is any single trick in mingling that works so well, so easily, and so often as having your own mingling prop of some kind. While purists might cast a scornful eye on the use of these obvious and common mingling crutches, I believe that anything that helps you have a good time at a party is legit:

○ *the coolest, newest, smallest cell phone or camera phone*

○ *a digital camera*

○ *a Blackberry, Sidekick, or Treo or other PDA*

○ *iPods, iDogs, or any other kind of small iThing*

○ *a Swiss Army knife*

○ *an unusual pen*

○ *a SwissMemory (a Swiss Army knife with a USB memory stick attached)*

○ *a baby or small child (a newborn baby, should you happen to have one with you at the party, is of course the perfect foil; however, the conversation will be mostly limited to the child, and when the crying starts, the conversation will stop)*

○ *a purse dog (small dogs serve almost the same purpose as babies but can be just as much trouble)*

The Hors D'oeuvre Maneuver

If you feel as though you need some kind of prop, but you've neglected to bring one with you, it may be the right time for the Hors D'oeuvre Maneuver. This technique is somewhat brazen, but it serves two purposes: It provides you with a piece of conversation, and it helps you move around the room freely.

You may be someone who has always had trouble circulating from one group to another and would like to try it with some mingling training wheels. First, offer your services to your host or hostess to pass a tray of food throughout the room. Try to select the yummiest items from the buffet table, and then just set off into the room. You won't have to worry about opening lines. Believe me, the minute people see you coming with those goodies, they will open a path for you. In fact, if the food you are carrying is good enough, you can just stay in one place and end up with a crowd around you.

The best thing about this mingling method? It's automatic. Carrying a tray of food doesn't just *allow* you to mingle; it actually *forces* you to mingle, as it would be rude to the other guests for you to stay too long with one group of people.

Drawbacks: People may mistake you for one of the hired help. Also, you may find that the conversation while you and your tray are present in the group is limited to the food. In other words, people may associate you too much with the food and not want to segue into other topics while you are standing there with your tray. Most important: If you are passing food, you can't be eating it at the same time. Eating off the tray you are passing is impolite. This can end up being too much torture to be worth it!

Working the Bar or Food Area

When asked what is the first thing they do upon arriving at a party, almost everyone I know has the same answer: They get something to eat or drink. I usually do the same thing myself. It's perfectly natural. But make sure you recognize the bar or food area not just as a place to sate your hunger or thirst but as a vibrant mingling center, complete with props and pitfalls.

I myself fell into one of those pitfalls at a Christmas party. The food table was laden with various delicacies; and my undoing was some particularly exquisite smoked salmon placed at the head of the table. Smoked salmon is a passion of mine, and I'm ashamed to say I get quite greedy when I'm around it. I was doing a little mingling but more or less hovering over the salmon until I got an uneasy feeling I couldn't quite put my finger on. I mused over it as I took my tenth piece of salmon. Then it hit me. Instead of using the food area for mingling purposes, I had been using my mingling ability to get to the food! Specifically, to get to the salmon.

Never forget that your primary goal is mingling; food and drink should be a secondary part of your fun. They also can facillitate conversation. Here are a few simple rules for when you mingle in the food or bar area:

1. **Don't camp out by the bar or buffet.** Not only could you end up getting tipsy or sick (or both), but also it isn't considerate. Some people won't have a chance to get near the bar or buffet if others won't move away. This rule is most important with respect to the bar. I know too many people who use their own minglephobia as an excuse to stand by the bar and guzzle drinks. Soon they find they have enough confidence to talk to anybody. But will anybody want to talk to them?

2. **Offer to help others get food or drink.** If you are standing next to each other, it's an excellent mingling ploy to help another person in some small way, even holding a drink for the person while he or she cuts a piece of cheese. It endears you to the other person, shows you are a nice guy, and that person more or less has to talk to you a little afterward or risk being discourteous.

3. **Talk about the food and the presentation.** Party food makes for great, safe conversation. Talk about any unusual foods; ask another person if she knows what's in the dip or to recommend something. But don't overdo it. Let the subject of the food eventually lead you somewhere else.

4. **Avoid making negative comments about any of the food unless the other person says something first.** You never know who is responsible for the cooking. Even if you are positive that no one at the party made any of the food, you could inadvertently insult someone; the dish could be exactly like one the person you're talking to makes at home or brought to someone else's party last week.

5. **Try not to point with food or gesture with drinks.** It's unattractive and accidents can happen. Someone might get a bread stick in his ear.

6. **Make good use of the time you are in a line for food or drink.** Lines are great places for conversations (see p. 161). They also happen to be the one place where it doesn't look funny if you *aren't* talking to anyone. If you're lucky, you'll have someone to talk to while waiting, but if not, you can use the time to scope out the party and map out a mingling campaign.

PLAYING DOUBLES: TEAM MINGLING

The best mingling prop you can have is another person. While it is definitely not advisable to stick like glue to your spouse or friend at a party, a partner can be a great asset if used properly. Regrettably, many partners fail to take advantage of this teaming-up opportunity—or even to recognize the potential power they have as party allies. Over the years I have listened to countless complaints about partners at parties: husbands who mysteriously disappear only to be discovered off in a bedroom reading a book; friends who attach themselves to the people who brought them, never leaving them alone for a second; business partners who won't pull their weight in working a room full of clients; and wives who stand in a corner, too shy to mingle with anyone. More commonly, there is the couple who go to a party and stand there talking only to each other.

The basic premise of team mingling is *not* to mingle as a pair. You already see each other enough, and you won't meet as many people if you hang out together. Moreover, you will have a much better time, I promise you, if you venture off on your own. Split up, even if you come back to each other now and then to recharge.

However, mingling separately doesn't mean you shouldn't help each other. Teammates back each other up. And because you know each other well, there are numerous ways you can enhance each other's mingling adventure—to double your power, double your fun.

Preparty Strategy Sessions

Preparty strategy sessions can be very constructive, especially for business partners. Before the event you might discuss what contacts may be present and which one of you is going to schmooze whom. Also, you can decide which of you is better at what (Is one of you a great greeter? Is the other one better at entertaining people?), then encourage each other in what you each do best. In most couples one person is a better mixer than the other. This person is going to have to do more to help the less confident mingler. It is very much like playing doubles in tennis: If your backhand is weak, let your partner cover for you; if you're better at the net, then you need to adjust your stance accordingly. Determine how you can take the best advantage of your coupledom.

Conversational Procurement

This is a good technique for helping out a truly timid partner or friend. It may sound a bit complicated but will be well worth mastering if your partner suffers from minglephobia. Basically, the idea is to lead as many people as you can—like sacrificial offerings—to your partner. Figuratively speaking, what you are going to do is hand-feed him or her a virtual feast of conversations.

Step One: Let's say your wife has wallflower-itis. Upon entering the party scene, first guide your wife to someone you both know or introduce yourself and your wife to someone as soon as possible. (We'll call this hypothetical person Mack.) Try to get your wife involved in the conversation right away—using common conversational ploys such as, "My wife feels exactly the same way, don't you, honey?" "Mack, you must tell my wife about the time you . . . ," or, "Get my wife to explain that; she's the only one I know who understands it!" Always be as complimentary to her as you can without embarrassing her, to help build up her confidence.

Step Two: Excuse yourself for a brief period of time. Go get a drink or some food for the two of you or put your coats in the other room. This will be your wife's trial separation. Make sure you *do* return to her in five minutes or so with the promised drink or food. She must feel from the start that you are watching out for her and that you will never leave her alone for very long.

Step Three: If, on the one hand, your wife and Mack are miraculously still chatting by the time you get back, give your wife an encouraging signal in the way of some kind of physical gesture (a slight squeeze of her shoulders, a hand on her waist) and say, "Excuse me, honey, excuse me, Mack, I've got to say hello to Georgie, but I'll be right back." You then leave your wife with the accommodating Mack for the time being. If, on the other hand, Mack has escaped from your wife before you can return with the drinks, you then take her over to another person or group, get the conversation going as before, then leave her there.

Step Four: From this point on, you will be bringing people over to your wife throughout the evening. For example, let's say you have been talking to a man for about ten minutes—perhaps he is regaling you about the latest developments in genetic testing. Wait for him to take a breath, then say, "I'm sorry, but my wife has *got* to hear this. She was just asking me about this the other night. I think she read the same article in the paper." Take him by the arm and physically lead him to your wife. Introduce them, and you're off again with a casual, "Be right back." (This is technically not a lie as you *will* be back, again and again, delivering to your mate a constant stream of people with whom to converse.) Ideally, as the party goes on you will have to feed your wife less and less, as she adapts to fending for herself.

Intraparty Play Dates

You may have a husband who is so uninterested in mingling that it takes too much energy to assist him. Or maybe he didn't want to go to the party in the first place, but you forced him to come. It's frustrating to try to help someone mingle who really doesn't want to . . . so don't. Instead, try to locate a similarly disposed antimingler and sit your nonmingling partner down with him. (When in doubt just pick someone who looks as if he *may* also be a party pooper.) The idea is to find someone *else* who seems repelled by the idea of mingling with a lot of people, someone who would therefore happily commit to a long sit-down conversation in a quiet nook somewhere. By matching your hermitlike husband up with a kindred spirit, you ensure that he is— at least in a small way—participating in the party. It may not be a perfect solution, but it's certainly more appropriate than his being all alone in another room reading Proust.

Shepherding

If you happen to have a pathologically antisocial partner, one who re- sists even one-on-one interaction and who will actually disappear into the host's study to sit himself down with a book, you may have to physically shoo him back into the mingling pool. Shepherding is a beefed-up version of what you probably already do, that is, to inter- mittently go find your partner and herd him back into the party. What will help you, however, is to enlist other shepherds to aid you so that you don't have to personally check up on him every ten min- utes. Entreat one or two acquaintances to alternate with you in seek- ing out your lost sheep and firmly guiding him back to the main room under the guise of his being introduced to someone. Believe it or not, if the misanthrope is continually driven back to the party, he will eventually learn that his solitude is an impossibility. You may even find him returning to the party all on his own.

Reconnaissance and Rescue

Even the most confident people can (and usually do) use this form of team mingling, which consists mostly of an exchange of information. (It's like insider trading except that it isn't illegal.) It can be quite a handy thing to have an ally working the room with you; you can alert each other about mingling minefields and party pleasure points. With a word or two in her ear, you can help steer your mingling partner to the most interesting people, as well as help her avoid the most unin- teresting ones. You can point out the deadly bore or the sloppy drunk so she won't have to go through the same unpleasantness you just did. Your partner can help *you* avoid the faux pas she has made; if she's just asked the host whether the young woman at his side was his daughter home from college only to discover the woman is his new girlfriend, your partner can save you from making the same blunder. You and your "teammate" can provide each other with names either of you may have forgotten. Throughout the party, you can check in with each other to see how it's going and to see if there is someone else present whom you need to give a little mingle to. Many couples even have signals they give each other when they want to be rescued from a person. (Try to be subtle—patting yourself on the head while rubbing your stomach isn't recommended.) Usually a discreet movement of the eyes and raise of the brows will do it. *Warning:* Be very careful when whispering to each other about people at the party. It's a well-known component of Murphy's Law that whenever you say something really mean about someone, that someone is always standing right behind you.

The Mating Call

For this trick you don't even need the help of your partner, just the *fact* of him. This common escape technique is a couples version of the Counterfeit Search escape (see p. 77). In this form of the Search, you make it obvious to the person or people you're itching to ditch that your mate is asking you to join him or her. If the ditchee knows who your spouse is, you can execute the Mating Call without using words; you can merely roll your eyes in the direction of your mate as if to say, *He's calling me again!* Or nod or wave in the direction of your mate, appearing to answer his or her call. If, however, the subject is *not* familiar with your mate, you can say, "Oh . . . pardon me, my wife wants me . . . excuse me for a moment, will you?" The "for a moment" is a nice touch and can soften the exit. It implies you really would like to come back to continue the conversation, but it isn't a promise. The brilliant thing about the Mating Call? It indicates you are leaving against your will, so it protects the ditchee's feelings. You just look loyal, at best, or henpecked, at worst.

Watching a good team at a party—two people who've been mingling together for many years—is like watching older couples on the dance floor. There is an in-sync, effortless quality about a good mingling duo. Mingling separately, they can seem more "together" than if they were circulating as a pair.

6 Under Fire: Handling Unusual Situations

LIE OR DIE

Let's say you memorize fifty brilliant opening lines and you have all the right props; let's say you even master the Butterfly Flit. Now you're an expert in the art of mingling, right? Not necessarily. The true test of whether you are a good mingler lies not in what you do under normal circumstances but in what you do in an emergency. Being able to handle yourself well in unexpected or unusual mingling situations takes concentration, imagination, flexibility, and—by far the most important ingredient—the unhesitating, unwavering ability to lie *through your teeth*. I can't stress enough how important the white lie is in mingling, especially when you are faced with imminent disaster of some kind. It can be absolutely essential to your survival. Remember: You're on the mingling battlefield, facing impossible odds, fierce opposition, near calamity. You never know what you'll be asked to handle. While your course of action may or may not call for a friendly fib, it's important to know from the start that when the moment of truth arrives, you may have to . . . lie or die.

DEALING WITH FAUX PAS

You are at an art gallery opening; your escort is a close friend of the artist whose work is being shown. After mingling for over an hour with various groups of people, you return to talk to a woman with whom you have chatted previously but to whom you have not been formally introduced. You remark to her that while you find the paintings somewhat interesting, you don't really "get what it's all about." Then you ask her, "So, are you an artist, too?" She responds somewhat coolly, "Actually, this is *my* opening."

We've all made embarrassing errors while mingling; I have made some real doozies myself. And yet each time it happens, each time we're faced with that excruciating moment right after the faux pas when we wish we could just disappear into the floorboards, we're convinced that no one has ever been so stupid or so clumsy before.

How many times has the following happened to you?

- *calling someone you know by the wrong name*

- *being overheard gossiping by the person who is the object of the gossip*

- *bumping into someone or spilling something on someone*

- *bringing up a subject you immediately realize had been a secret*

- *talking about last night's great party to which persons present weren't invited*

- *loudly mistaking someone's wife or husband for his or her daughter or son*

- *asking a nonexpectant woman about her pregnancy*

- *broaching a taboo topic of conversation*

Whether you've just stepped on someone's foot with your spike heel or inquired as to the whereabouts of someone's dead husband, try to remember two things: Everyone makes faux pas, even the person to whom you've just done the damage; and there's always a way to recover (at least partially) from any snafu and to make the best of a bad situation. The important thing is not to fold under the pressure of your social blunder but instead deal with it and learn from it. Faux pas build mingling character, and if you don't run away from them, they can help to make you a much stronger conversationalist.

When You're Dressed Wrong

If you've ever walked into a room full of tuxedos and evening gowns in a tweed skirt and knee-highs, as I have, you have experienced the particular vise of horror that grips you when you realize you're dressed all wrong for the party. I'm not talking here about having on a turtleneck instead of a tie; I mean when you are dressed noticeably, definitely *wrong*.

When you find yourself in this situation, you have several choices. *Please note:* I am assuming here that the fact that you're dressed wrong bothers you; naturally, if you are either confident enough or enlightened enough not to care, you won't think of this as a faux pas and the following advice doesn't apply.

Your first option is, of course, to leave. Turn right around and walk out, rent a movie, and spend a quiet night at home, convinced it was fate and you would have had a lousy time anyway. But I emphatically do not condone this course of action. It's giving up.

Your second option is to dash home and change into an appropriate outfit. If you think you can pull this off, by all means, go for it. But be sure to get out before anybody sees you, or your "Before" and "After" show might be more embarrassing than merely being dressed wrong. Also, the logistics of getting home, changing your clothes, and getting back to the party before it's over may be overwhelming. The stressfulness of all that running back and forth may not be worth it. It's bound to put you in a bad mood.

The third choice: Pretend nothing is wrong with the way you are dressed. In your mind you must see yourself dressed in completely appropriate clothing, then just mingle as you normally would. But don't forget what happened to the emperor in "The Emperor's New Clothes." All it takes is for one person to say to you, "Did you forget this was black-tie?" and the illusion could be shattered.

Your fourth option: You can use humor, the universal antidote for faux pas. For instance, if you are in casual clothes and everyone else is in formal dress, you can say in mock amazement, "Look how many people are inappropriately dressed; imagine anyone wearing a tux to an affair like this!" As always with humor, it has to be funny; if you don't think you can pull it off, don't attempt it.

Your fifth and last option, and the one I *do* suggest you choose, is this. *Turn your inappropriate appearance into an interesting story.* This way, you take the hand that's been dealt to you and bluff it out. Imagine you arrive in a gray business suit and blue shirt at your friend Karen's house and, upon entering, you realize everyone is in black tie except for you. Suddenly you remember: the invitation *did* say formal, but you had such a bad day at the office it went right out of your head. But you don't panic. You know that before you begin to mingle, before you talk to anyone, all you have to do is to take the time to decide what your story is going to be. You remain in the coatroom or foyer for a minute, until you are ready.

You confidently enter the fray. After your opening line, you indicate your attire and say laughingly, "Can you believe this? Ol' Karen really got me this time. She neglected to inform me about it being black-tie. I pulled the same trick on her two years ago and we've been paying each other back ever since." This leads you and the other person into a discussion of practical jokes and of how you both know the hostess. You've successfully turned your inappropriate dress into usable subject matter.

Admittedly, this is a rather bold lie, as it involves fabricating something untrue about the hostess. (It usually is not a good idea to tell lies about other people.) But Karen, if she is a friend of yours, won't mind this innocent ruse, even if she does hear about it, which is highly unlikely. A less outrageous story might be that you have just gotten off a train or plane and didn't have time to go home first. Or you can say that you've been locked out of your apartment, or that the cleaners burned down (along with all your dressy clothes), or that a jealous ex-lover has been stealing all your mail and you never received the actual invitation. Whatever tale you choose to tell, make it intriguing. Remember, your objective is not merely to re-cover from your fashion faux pas but to make it work for you, to turn it into a mingling aid, just like wearing an accessory or bringing a prop.

As you can imagine, it's easier to pull this off if you are over-dressed rather than underdressed, like when you're wearing a tux and everyone else is in jeans. Then you simply adopt the position that you are going (or have already gone) to some very fancy, chic affair other than the current one.

A final note: Don't forget to consider telling the truth before you decide on a lie. But only if the truth is as interesting as a made-up story would be. If the truth is that you just made a stupid mistake for no particular reason, stick to deceit. This isn't Sunday school; this is a party!

Introductions: A Recurring Nightmare

The problem of being awkward with introductions is not unusual. In fact, 99.999 percent of us have some trouble in this area. You may be uncertain about whether to introduce someone using the first name, last name, or both, about whether or not to use a qualifier ("this is my accountant"), even about whether or not it is in fact your responsibility to introduce two people in a given situation. However, all of this is small potatoes compared with the seemingly inevitable mingling night-mare of having to introduce someone *whose name you have forgotten.*

Flubbing names during introductions is such a common faux pas that some experts have given this particular lack of social grace a clinical term: "dysnomnesia." Dysnomnesia afflicts everyone at one time or another. Either you can't remember the person's name, you use an incorrect qualifier (e.g., ". . . and this is her husband" when the two people are not married), or you actually start a con-versation before you realize you have mistaken the person for someone else.

Whatever form your greeting goof takes, one thing is certain: The more important it is that you get it right, the more likely it is that you are going to screw up in some frightful way. So whether you've just forgotten your boss's name or your own, here are some recovery lines that may help alleviate the situation:

○ *"I'm so sorry; I have a name disorder. Really. I've been diagnosed by a name disorder specialist—Dr. . . . Dr. . . . I can't remember his name!"*

○ *"I've never been able to remember names; it runs in my family. At family reunions there is generally a lot of 'Hey, yous.'"*

○ *"Whoops, I'm afraid I thought you were Bob Tompkins. Well, we were obviously meant to talk together. There are no accidents in life, right?"*

It's one thing to forget people's names if you've met them only once or twice or if you haven't seen them in a while. But all too often it's someone whose name you really should know and who is going to be insulted to find out you don't. In other words, a faux pas in the making. This is absolute agony when it happens, and I've watched hundreds of minglers try to deal with it in different ways, ranging from apologizing exuberantly ("Oh *God*, I'm so sorry, *jeez*, wow, I can't *believe* this, I can't *believe* I've forgotten your name!") to throwing up their hands and walking away. But there are better ways to deal with this kind of mental slip. Next time you draw a blank while making introductions, try one of the following ploys:

1. **Manipulate them into introducing themselves.** This is the smoothest and most effective way to handle your memory lapse. When it's done well, no one will ever suspect you. If you have forgotten one person's name in the group, turn to that person first and smile. Then turn invitingly to a person whose name you *do* remember and say, "This is Linden Bond," turning back casually toward the forgotten person. The person whose name you haven't mentioned yet will automatically (it's a reflex) say, "Nice to meet you, Linden; I'm Sylvia Cooper," and usually offer a hand to shake. If you are trying to introduce two people and you can't remember *either* of their names, your problem is more serious. Still you can usually get away with simply saying, "Have you two met each other?" If you smile confidently and wait, the two will introduce themselves (though those few seconds while you're waiting can seem like a lifetime). At the very worst it will appear as if your introduction skills are a bit sloppy, but no one will be able to tell you've forgotten their names.

2. **Confess, then dwell on it.** Here's another example of turning a faux pas to your advantage. What you do is admit you've forgotten the name(s), apologizing sincerely. After the introductions are over, let the mishap lead you into a discussion of why it is

harder for some people to remember names than others (the left-brain/right-brain theory, the male/female theory, etc.). It may help you to keep in mind that almost everyone has a bad memory when it comes to names and yet almost everyone thinks it's a unique failing. Using your own social error as subject matter shows that you are comfortable with your mistake; you don't feel that guilty about it. And since people tend to believe whatever you project, no one will hold a grudge.

3. **Introduce them using something besides their names.** Names and labels are highly overrated in our society anyway. Why not say instead, "Jody, I want you to meet a woman after your own heart!" Then you just present the other person, who will offer her name or not. You can also cover up any uneasiness you have about your forgetting names by using flattery: "I want you to meet the most fascinating person at the party!" or, "You two should really meet—seeing as how you're both so gorgeous!" If you lay it on thick, it puts up a smoke screen and nobody will notice you've forgotten their names. Or if they do, they won't care anymore!

Storytelling as a Healing Technique

Introduction problems are one thing, but what about the really bad faux pas? How can you deal with that horrible, sinking terror that engulfs you right after one of those conversation-stopping social blunders, such as when the hostess overhears you telling someone that the only reason you came to her party was because you had nothing else to do? It's not easy to go on after one of these disasters until you do something to help heal the social wound you've inadvertently inflicted.

Keep in mind that everyone, at one time or another, makes fools of themselves while mingling. In fact, if you never made any mistakes, socially, you'd never improve your mingling skills. Taking risks, at least occasionally, is necessary to your mingling growth—I might even go so far as to say it is necessary to your social health. Because everyone knows what it feels like to make a faux pas, everyone is just as anxious as the one who has committed the social sin to see him recover. They want the tension to pass as much as he does. It is for this reason, I think, that Storytelling is such an effective way of mending the mingling faux pas.

The first thing you need for this technique is a really good faux pas story. The idea is to tell the witnesses of your current faux pas about something you did at another time that was *more* embarrassing than whatever it is you have just done. Ideally, it should be something that actually happened to you or to someone you know, because in the wake of whatever terrible social error you've committed you have to be open and sincere in order to reestablish your position in the group. If told convincingly, your story will do much to dispel the humiliation surrounding you.

I confess I make faux pas often, especially while trying out new lines and maneuvers, but I have a great faux pas story—a true one— which almost always acts as a healing ointment for any mistakes I may have made. What I usually do, in the midst of the embarrassing silence or the nervous laughter I have caused, is say something like, "I really can't believe I just did that [said that]. Boy, leave it to me! Did I ever tell you about the time I . . ." And I recount my Erica Jong story.

Years ago when I was looking for a job, someone arranged for me to have an interview with Erica Jong, for the position of her secretarial assistant. At that time I was very nervous to be meeting a famous author, and it didn't help that I had broken my foot and was on crutches. On top of everything else, it was raining on the evening of the interview and I couldn't get a cab. By the time I arrived at Ms. Jong's

Upper East Side town house—my hair dripping wet, my crutches muddy—I was almost an hour late for the interview. I was a complete wreck. What a way to begin! But I took a deep breath and rang the doorbell.

The housekeeper let me in, and then the fabulous Erica Jong herself came sweeping down the front stairs. She graciously put out her hand.

"Hello, I'm Erica Jong, " she said to me, smiling.

I looked straight into her eyes, smiled back at her, and said, "Hello, I'm Erica Jong."

(!)

In my nervousness and general disarray, I had actually introduced myself as *her*! There was a long, long moment of the loudest silence I have ever experienced—all three of us, I think, were totally confused—until Ms. Jong came through for both of us like the mingling pro she must be and reminded me gently, "You must be Jeanne Martinet."

"Uh . . . yes, that's who I am," I agreed sheepishly.

I don't think there are many moments (certainly I haven't had many) in life that can rival the embarrassment of the one I just described; however, the incident did end up serving a very useful purpose: *It gets me out of faux pas hot water almost every time.* After I tell that story, no one thinks too much about whatever current error I may have committed.

When using a personal anecdote as a healing tool, remember: It is better if you are the faux pas *perpetrator* in the tale you tell; it's not as effective to tell a story about someone else messing up. It can sound as if you are trying to compare your faux pas favorably to someone else's (although if the story is outstanding in some way, it can work). Also, you can use Storytelling to help someone *else* recover from a faux pas ("Hey, don't worry about it; let me tell you about the time I . . ."). This is the ultimate mingling move: In one fell swoop you've been kind to a fellow human being, endeared yourself to him or her for at least the remainder of the party, taken control of the conversation, and found a reason to tell one of your favorite stories!

Disclaimer: Storytelling won't work in every situation, of course. If you've just spilled hot coffee on someone's blouse, that person is probably not going to stick around while you tell a story.

All-Purpose Faux Pas Recovery Lines

If you don't have a good story to tell or if the faux pas isn't conducive to Storytelling, you may be able to use one of the following recovery lines to regain your balance. Quick recovery lines are also invaluable to those people who are so paralyzed after a faux pas that a short line or two is all they are able to utter:

○ *"Just testing."*

○ *"Sorry, it's a line I read somewhere."*

○ *"Did I say that out loud?*

○ *"Let's run that scene over."*

○ *"OK. So I need some lessons in mingling."*

○ *"I'm on automatic pilot tonight, and I think I just crashed!"*

○ *"Excuse me. Another personality took over my body there for a minute."*

○ *"Um, is there a time machine anywhere around?"*

○ *"Forgive me; I'm afraid I'm not feeling at all well."*

○ *"I'm terribly sorry; I'm afraid your beauty short-circuited me."*

○ *"Arrggh! Somebody up there must hate me!"*

○ "I always wondered what would happen if I ever really embarrassed myself. . . . I'm still alive. Good."

○ "That was my evil twin: Skippy."

The Faux Pas Moi: The Art of Denial

Sometimes the wisest course of action is to refute the crime. In the Faux Pas Moi, the idea is to deny the very occurrence of the faux pas. It may seem like a dangerous ploy, but the payoff can be big, and it is worth attempting when you are caught in truly horrible faux pas situations where the idea of trying to apologize or make excuses is not a palatable one.

There are four different ways to play out the Faux Pas Moi:

1. **Pretend you were misunderstood.** Suppose you commit a pretty bad faux pas, such as insulting a play or a book without realizing the person to whom you are waxing critical is the author. You have been chatting away in a group and the conversation turns to a play that recently opened, a play called *The Horrible Mistake,* and you say something like, "Oh, I saw that play; boy, it really dragged!"

   To your intense dismay the man to your right gives you an irritated look and says to you, "Oh really? I didn't think it dragged when I wrote it."

   Sudden disaster. OK. Take a second to breathe. Remain calm. Do not allow your humiliation to show on your face. Instead, look puzzled, and quickly think of the name of another play that is currently running.

   "So you're the author of *Mayhem on 42nd Street?*" you say. "Really? I thought a woman wrote that." Now, the playwright may be suspicious and suspect you are just trying to cover up your gaffe. However, the real trick to the successful Faux Pas Moi is sticking to your denial position and refusing to cave in. Just say to yourself: *Deny, deny, deny.* It's like poker; you can't start to bluff and then change your mind halfway through the hand. (If you are not ready to go all the way with it, don't try this type of recovery at all.)

At this point, the playwright will probably answer you dubiously with something like, "No, I wrote *The Horrible Mistake*," as if to say, *Don't try to get out of it now,* but remember: You must not fold! Keep insisting, "But I was talking about *Mayhem on 42nd Street.* Isn't that what Joe was just talking about?" This is a great technique when it works; sometimes you can manage to totally erase the mistake. The worst that can happen is that you "muff the bluff" and you are really not much worse off than you were before. After all, the injured playwright expects you to try to recover from such a blunder; the whole incident would probably be *more* insulting to him if you didn't make the effort. But hopefully he will believe your fervent denial. (His ego will want him to, in any case.)

2. **Blame someone else.** This may seem unethical, especially if we are talking about blaming a push or a drink spill on another person present. (But don't rule it out. All's fair in love and embarrassment.) However, remember that you can often blame an anonymous person. For example, in the case of the preceding playwright fiasco, you could try this: "Oh *no*! You're the playwright? Oh my gosh. You're not going to believe this now, I know, but I never even *saw* the play. I was just trying to contribute to the conversation. I heard some doofus on the bus talking about it. Boy, that's the last time I pretend someone else's opinion is mine."

3. **Pretend you were only kidding.** Perhaps you are talking to a woman you haven't seen in a while. Fatigue or alcohol or boredom has made you careless, and you say to her something like, "So, what ever happened to that weirdo you used to date?" The minute the words leave your lips you have a bad feeling. And sure enough, she answers with a cold smile, "I married him."

Here's what you do: Keep that smile on your face; laugh, if you can. Even put your arm around the woman for added effect, and say with appropriate merriment, "I know that, silly! [Name of mutual friend at party] just told me. So where is he tonight?" If the person still looks offended: "Hey, can't you take a joke? Didn't you know I was kidding?"

4. **Completely ignore it.** You have to be a cool customer to pull this off, but if you can do it, it's a no-muss/no-fuss way of effecting the Faux Pas Moi. Here's what you do—or rather, what you don't do: Don't flinch; don't laugh; don't blush; don't acknowledge the faux pas in any way. Just erase it from your reality. It didn't happen. You didn't say it. You never did it. If you can act innocent enough, sometimes other people will begin to think they imagined the faux pas or at least that whatever it was, wasn't any big deal.

This form of the Faux Pas Moi is not just for daredevils; it is also for people who are too chicken or stunned to do anything about what has just taken place. Actually, the Faux Pas Moi is sometimes the easiest—maybe the only—dignified way to deal with what's happened.

For example, one day a woman I know named Sally went to one of those terribly cute restaurants where the rest rooms have confusing, arty symbols on them (often in the form of super-stylized hats or shoes) and so it was through no great fault of her own that she found herself suddenly . . . in the men's room.

As soon as she entered, she saw a surprised (and occupied) man standing at a urinal. Sally felt that she had already come too far inside to leave gracefully. And so, unruffled, without blinking an eye, and ignoring the man's astonished stare, Sally quickly walked right up to one of the sinks, washed her hands, dried them with a paper towel, and walked back out. (She then proceeded to locate the women's room, where there was—naturally!—a long waiting line.)

Admittedly, Sally's boldness is an extreme illustration of the Faux Pas Moi but it serves as a reminder that we must never underestimate the power we have at all times to create our own reality.

The Faux Pas-cifist

If there's one thing that warms my heart about the human race, it's watching a Faux Pas-cifist, or faux pas angel, at work. A Faux Pas-cifist is a witness, a bystander, or a third party who assesses a faux pas situation and steps in unselfishly to save the day. Of course, often the faux pas victim herself is kind enough to help the faux pas perpetrator over any embarrassment, but it's another thing altogether when an individual who would otherwise not be directly involved offers assistance. These people are no less than the heroes and heroines of the social universe.

A few years ago my friend Barbie and I were having a very intense tête-à-tête while standing in a crowd outside a lecture hall in Chelsea. Now, when you live in New York City you get used to discussing the intimate details of your life in the midst of strangers, because frankly, if you didn't you'd never talk anywhere but inside your apartment. You learn how to think of strangers both as people and as part of the scenery; you tend to ignore the fact that in this crowd twenty people could be listening to every word you say. Unfortunately, this practice can sometimes lead to trouble and in this case caused me to forget one of the major rules of avoiding faux pas—namely: *Be aware at all times of who is within earshot.*

I was filling Barbie in on a date I had had with a delicious guy who worked in the financial industry but also cooked and taught yoga. Just when I was saying, "Richard is really nice, seems really centered and healthy and all, except the one thing I can't figure out is that all his friends I met at this party we went to were so *incredibly* boring," I happened to turn around and glance at the man behind me, who looked vaguely familiar and was, of course, none other than one of the incredibly boring friends in question. (Oh, when will I ever learn that New York is just another small town?) There was no doubt in my mind that he had heard me; he was wearing a very hurt, angry expression and looked the other way when I looked at him.

When I realized that not only had I insulted this man but that also he had heard me gushing on and on about my date with his friend, I felt like knocking myself on the head until I was unconscious. I just sank into Barbie, closed my eyes, and put my head on her shoulder, too mortified to try to perform the Faux Pas Moi or any other recovery technique. I felt completely and utterly doomed. The worst thing was that we were trapped in the crowd, so I couldn't even make a quick exit.

Luckily for me, however, the woman who was with the "boring man" suddenly stepped forward. "Excuse me," she said, tapping me on the shoulder. I had no alternative; I turned around. "I think I met you at the party on Saturday." She smiled and went on in a very composed manner. "I couldn't help overhearing what you were saying— you know, big parties really *can* be boring, especially if you don't know anybody there." She smiled again. Both the boring man and I hung on to her every word; she was our lifeline. She smiled even wider and said, "Especially if you are with someone new who you really want to get to know. Richard *is* really nice, isn't he?" I blushed but smiled back, gratefully. Then she indicated the boring man. "Did you meet Joe?" Blushing even deeper, I mumbled, "I don't think so." I introduced Barbie, and then this fabulous Faux Pas-cifist, whose name turned out to be Lila, led us all in a nice four-way conversation. Joe was stiff at first, but I made sure I was especially nice to him and acted supremely interested in everything he said. By the time the crowd began moving back into the lecture hall I felt that Joe believed that I did not really think he was boring and that he knew I was not a total grouthead and he was not going to run and tell Rich that I was one. Considering the enormity of the faux pas, it was a major—if not total—recovery, and I owed it all to Lila.

Lila was a master Faux Pas-cifist. There are not that many people who could and would handle such a situation with as much finesse and generosity. Most Faux Pas-cifists are lesser but still admirable people who might help others recover from faux pas using a simple recovery line ("Don't mind Charley; he's a new parent—he's had about five seconds' sleep today"). I've seen a lot of people who have enough presence of mind to save another person from a common faux pas situation like an introduction problem. The Faux Pas-cifist simply takes over for someone who is floundering and fills in the missing name(s) or qualifier(s). Another typical strategy of your garden-variety Faux Pas-cifist is one of diversion; the kind interloper sees someone in trouble and fills the awkwardness with a change of subject or a witty comment.

All forms of Faux Pas-cifism are godsends. I try to be a Faux Pas-cifist whenever possible and you should, too. With the kindness of strangers—as well as a bag full of recovery tricks—we will all be able to survive whatever the faux pas fates hand us.

NEGOTIATING TOUGH ROOMS

Every time you set out to go to a party, you are entering the world of the Unknown. It's important to be prepared for any scenario—to be ready to adapt the basic rules of mingling to fit—as you have no idea what may greet you once you get there.

The Sardine Can

Sometimes you are faced with what I like to call the Sardine Can. You arrive at a social function and discover it's wall-to-wall people. You hesitate at the door before going in; it seems like masochism to try to mingle in this teeming mass of humanity. You know that movement will be limited, fresh air scarce, and the line for the bathroom impossibly long. For some crazy reason, you go in anyway. (I know I always do.)

Once you've elected to become a sardine, here are some helpful tips on how best to proceed:

1. **Use the most direct openings and simplest subject matter in your mingling portfolio.** Crowded parties are invariably loud, so any kind of complicated communication is out. Forget trying anything that entails irony or nuance, for example. People aren't going to be able to hear you. I recommend the Honest Approach as an entrance maneuver for the Sardine Can; people are more or less resigned to the fact that since they can't move, they have to talk to whoever happens to be next to them. For this reason, you'll find it easier than usual to get into conversations. It's just hard to have them, in all the din!

2. **Keep your eye out for any people close to you who are making their way through the crowd.** This is your only hope of movement at a really packed party. If people are strong enough or determined enough to wade through the multitude, take advantage of the path they are cutting and follow in their wake. You don't even have to know exactly where you are going;

between the food, the bar, and the bathroom, you're bound to get closer to somewhere you want to be! This maneuver is much more extreme than Piggybacking; here it's OK if you actually physically hang on to people (as long as they don't mind). They probably won't even notice. When I see partygoers doing this well, it reminds me of how city drivers use a speeding ambulance or fire engine to get through heavy traffic.

3. **Don't worry about escape techniques.** While actual, physical movement may be limited, it's much easier to exit, psychologically speaking. The Sardine Can is a much more informal place, due to the decreased personal space. Rules of courtesy and etiquette are relaxed. Really crowded parties are so chaotic that people will hardly notice when you turn away from them. Even if you should happen to be in a one-on-one with an aggressive type who doesn't want to let you go, you won't lack for human sacrifices. Just reach out and grab someone, and hook him up with your creep.

4. **Smile a lot.** Facial expressions of all kinds are at a premium while you are in the Sardine Can. Since hearing is limited, body language has to take the place of verbal communication. (In fact, a working knowledge of sign language could be a plus.)

The Thin Room

It's a whole different kettle of fish when you arrive at an affair and find that there is practically no one there. It could be that you're early, in which case it's only a temporary Thin Room and you can wait it out. But if it's already an hour and a half after the party's official starting time, those five or six guests could be it. The rules of human kindness dictate that you remain—at least for a little while—since the hostess may be suicidal at this point. (She's not about to let you get away, in any case; she's probably locked the door after you.)

Here are some suggestions about how to handle the Thin Room:

1. **Encourage togetherness.** Probably the best time that can be had by all is if everyone stops trying to pretend it's a normal mingling situation. If there are only five people there, give up the structure of a cocktail party (where people are supposed to stand up and mingle) and help the hostess turn it into an intimate soiree instead (sit in chairs and on the sofa in a cozy circle). You should at least try to maneuver any separate groups closer together, for the simple reason that it is going to make it much easier for you to move between them. If you have a group of two people on one side of the room and a group of three way over on the other, it's going to be awkward to circulate. Having to walk by yourself across an empty room can make you self-conscious.

2. **Offer to get people things.** The fewer people there are, the more energy is needed to create a fun atmosphere. Help the hostess by making sure the few guests who are there are as happy as they can be. Your ulterior motive: Volunteering to assist the hostess gives you more freedom to move around quickly. In the Thin Room it's essential that you not get stuck with a dud or a bore for a long time—you could end up being the last two living souls at the party. The Thin Room can become the Empty Room in a blink of an eye.

3. **Use Playing a Game as much as possible.** Game playing (see chapter 3) can really help pep up a party. You should never, of course, suggest playing an actual party game like Charades or Dictionary without the express approval and encouragement

of the hostess (although nothing saves a Thin Room so much as a good game of Twister!).

4. **Bolster your hostess.** You may be disappointed that there aren't more people at the party, but just think how your hostess feels if people she invited didn't show. Since you can't do anything about the fact that this is a Thin Room, take this opportunity to make your hostess feel good about her party. Flatter the food; praise the decor; praise the gathering (the guests). In the Thin Room, it's vital that you project the positive. Everyone will appreciate it.

Mingling with Drunks

In almost every etiquette book ever written, from the early 1900s on, there is a section, usually written for the benefit of young ladies, on the proper and safe way to handle their inebriated gentlemen friends. In 1935, Alice-Leone Moats, in her famous *No Nice Girl Swears*, went so far as to categorize the different kinds of drunks: hilarious, lachrymose, loquacious, taciturn, argumentative, magisterial, belligerent, sentimental, amorous, and vomitous.

I rarely run into anything but the more benign type of drunk—the hilarious, the loquacious, the amorous, and the sentimental, all of which, depending on the level of inebriation, are easy to deal with (although I do know several people who fit into a separate category: the dangerously clumsy). If you *do* happen to find yourself up against one of the more unpleasant species of drunks, here are some guidelines:

○ **Never argue with a drunk.** It's useless. Humor the drunk, as you would a crazy person. But don't encourage him, either. If he says he is strong enough to lift you over his head, agree that he is certainly strong enough, but do not give him the opportunity to try it.

○ **Never flirt with a drunk.** You may as well play with matches near an open tub of gasoline. This applies to women drunks as well as men.

○ **Never tell a drunk you think he or she is drunk.** Unless the drunk's your friend, and even then it's best to wait until morning to discuss the evils of alcohol.

○ **Remember that you never have to mingle with a drunk unless you choose to.** It's the easiest thing in the world, usually, to escape from real drunks. Their senses are so dulled that you can use any escape technique you want and they'll never know what hit them. A lot of people seem to forget this and allow boring drunks to corner them for long periods of time. Don't buy into drunks' illusion that they are in control, mingling-wise (or any other wise). A simple "excuse me" and a hasty retreat is fine. Don't worry about leaving drunks standing all alone; they'll find someone else quickly enough. If you use the Human Sacrifice exit technique to escape from your drunk, try to find another drunk and sic them on each other. Otherwise, you could end up making enemies.

○ **If the drunk is really offensive, you can use the experience to your advantage at the party.** Remember the Helpless Hannah Ploy, where you asked people for help in order to have something to talk about? When you are being bothered by a heavy-duty drunk, you can have any number of people protecting you from the drunk, whether you are male or female. Remember the old Chinese proverb: Once someone saves your

life, he is responsible for it forever. (Translation: Once someone saves you from a drunk, he has basically adopted you and
will have to welcome you into whatever group he may be in
later.)

○ **Warn your host about a bad drunk.** By "bad drunk" I mean
someone who is getting violent or who is unsteady enough to
damage property or chase away the other guests. "Live and let
live" is a good philosophy, in most cases; after all, you are there
to mingle, not to be a policeman. But it's nice to alert the host to
a potential problem, so that he can decide whether or not he
wants to try to do anything about it.

One last piece of advice on this subject. If there are a lot of inebriated people at the party, cut your mingling short and go home. Or go
straight to the bar and order a double martini.

Mingling with the Truly Arrogant

For nearly all of the many social situations one can imagine, my advice is to try to be as positive and friendly as possible. But when mingling with the Truly Arrogant, there is only one path open to you: *Be
tough and treat 'em rough!*

Truly Arrogant people usually travel in packs, so you'll probably
have to deal with them in a group rather than just one here or there.
They can be country-club types, fashion designers, media people, or
the very rich. But in any case, they are hard to approach and often say
things like, "What a lovely little thing that is you've got on, darling. I
haven't seen anything like that in ages!"

Of course, if you have any sense and you have the option, you
should just go home. Truly Arrogant people are no fun to play with.
But sometimes, for whatever reasons, you're forced to stay and make

the best of it. Perhaps it's a business party and you're obligated to mingle; perhaps you're with a date and you don't want to make her leave. But whatever the reason, it may help if you remember a few simple rules for mingling with the Truly Arrogant:

1. **Make use of the survival fantasies** (see p. 2). If there is ever a time to use them, this is it. Mingling with the Truly Arrogant requires confidence.

2. **Breathe deeply.** This is always a good idea. It will help you to relax.

3. **Try not to flatter them.** Your first inclination will be to try to win them over by being nice. But Truly Arrogant people are usually superconfident, and confident people don't really respect flattery. In any case, flattery will give too much power to someone who is already assuming superiority.

4. **Tease the Truly Arrogant.** You have to try to communicate with them on their level first; show them you speak their language. Be careful, however. Your goal is bantering, not battering. This works best if you are dealing with members of the opposite sex. Tell them with a twinkle in your eye that you've heard something really terrible about them, or if they're celebrities, pretend you've never heard of them (or confuse them with some other celebrity who doesn't look at all like them). You've got to come on strong with these power mongers, and never let them see that it matters to you whether they like you or not.

However, once the Truly Arrogant start to warm up to you, once they begin to drop their snooty attitude, you must reward them by relenting and being nice to them. The rules for mingling with the

Truly Arrogant apply only for as long as they exhibit their arrogant behavior.

THE SIT-DOWN MINGLE

Sit-down dinners, as pleasant and socially complex as those occasions can be, do not fall under the category of mingling. What I'm talking about here are those times when you are at a large party and you make the fateful decision to sit down.

There are several reasons for sitting down at a party where most people are standing up. Either your feet are tired (an excellent reason), you want to escape from someone so you *pretend* your feet are tired (better make sure there's no space available next to you on the sofa); you've taken a heap of food from the buffet and are having trouble eating it while standing, or you would like to have a one-on-one conversation with someone without being interrupted. All of these are good reasons for taking a load off, but you should also be aware of the dangers of sitting.

The scariest thing about the Sit-Down Mingle is how difficult it can be to get back up. It is very hard to execute exit maneuvers from a sitting-down position. You could inadvertently sit next to a Venus Fly-trap, someone who has been lying in wait for someone to sit down next to her so she can tell them all about her recent gallbladder operation. Even if you sit down next to someone you know you'd love to talk to, that person could get up shortly after you've sat down, leaving you feeling publicly abandoned and, more important, leaving you wide open to the person you may have sat down to escape! You are taking a big risk when you sit down, so make sure it's really where you want to be.

The other, more insidious danger is a purely psychological one; once you are sitting down, you may lose your mingling momentum. You may find yourself thinking, *This is such a comfortable chair;*

maybe I'll just watch for the rest of the night. What's so great about talking to people anyway? Warning: If you feel yourself slipping into this state of mingleparalysis, get up! Immediately!

In order to master the Sit-Down Mingle, you have to learn how to get back on your feet. It's extremely hard to get free of someone (the Venus Flytrap, for example) who is really talking at you while you are both sitting down. She's basically got you where she wants you; you are her prisoner, or at least that's how it can feel to you.

Many of the normal escape techniques are problematic to perform from a sitting position; however, there are a couple techniques that I have found work pretty well. The first is a version of the Buffet Bye-Bye and Other Handy Excuses (see p. 73). Here an excuse you can use is the exact opposite of the one you probably used to sit down in the first place: you interrupt the person and say, "I'm sorry, but I have *got* to stand up. If I don't get up now, I never will." In the more polite form of this, you ask the Flytrap if she would like to stand up with you. If she says yes, then once you have her on her feet, you can use the Human Sacrifice (p. 71) or any number of other escape tactics to shake her off.

The Human Sacrifice also can be done from a sitting-down position, in this manner: Find someone nearby and get his attention. Try to bring him into the conversation a little; toss a few comments up at him; include him in whatever it is the Flytrap is talking about. The minute the new person even smiles at something you or the Flytrap says, start to get up, indicate your place, and say, "Would you care for a seat?" Now, depending on the new person's aspect as you stand, you may want to use the more aggressive, "Would you save my seat for a second?" This is a bit wicked, because it's almost impossible for him to refuse, but as I've said before, all's fair in love and mingling. (Of course, you *don't* come back. In fact, try not to be visible to that side of the room for the rest of the evening.) The Human Sacrifice from a chair is definitely a bold move to make, but at the worst, it's clunky.

It will always get you out of your seat, even if the Flytrap comes with you. Once you've begun your ascent, you can't be stopped.

One final word about the Sit-Down Mingle. Don't try it if you are extremely tired. There's only one thing I know of that's more impolite than getting drunk at a party, and that's falling asleep. Especially if you snore.

QUICK FIXES FOR DIRE CIRCUMSTANCES

How to React to Hand Kissing and Other Unwelcome Physicalities

On occasion, someone will get physical with you in a way that makes you feel uncomfortable—a kiss on the hand, an arm around the waist, a pat on the head, a kiss on the back of the neck (once, someone even pulled on my ear, I swear)—and you are not going to know what to do or say.

Every person's sense of physical boundaries is different. Some people can accept a hug or a kiss from a perfect stranger, while others see this as an almost criminal invasion of their personal space. Hand kissing is considered the height of chivalry by some and the height of insolence by others. For most people, however, when someone gets physical, it at least calls for some kind of comment. Whether you are flattered, embarrassed, or insulted, one of the following lines may come in handy. They are listed in order of most positive ("That was very nice") to most negative ("Try that again and I'll brain you"):

○ *"Why, thank you kindly, sir [madam]!"*

○ *"Chivalry is not dead!"*

○ *"Enchanté, monsieur."*

○ *"I'm not that kind of girl!" (Use this even if you are a man.)*

○ *"Must you do that?"*

○ *"Was that absolutely necessary?"*

○ *"Don't touch unless you're buying."*

○ *"Have you had your shots?"*

○ *"Excuse me, nobody informed me we had become intimate."*

○ *"Hey! I'm not Silly Putty, you know!"*

○ *"Sorry, babe, you're on private property."*

○ *"What do I look like to you—a grapefruit?" (Use only for hugs, squeezes, or pinches.)*

Handling Insults

The best story I ever heard about handling insults came from a friend of mine. I'll call him Tony (the name has been changed, for reasons that will be clear). It seems Tony was at a party where he was discussing a film he had just seen when a man who had been listening suddenly challenged him.

"You don't really mean to say you *enjoyed* that piece of garbage?" the man said to him in a snide voice.

Startled, Tony tried to defend himself: "Well . . . I mean it's not that I think it's great *art* or anything, but I thought it was entertaining, yes."

The man sneered. "Well, why would anybody in the film industry bother to make great art," the man said, "as long as there's pea-brains like you out there?"

Tony was absolutely stunned at the nastiness of this man, as were the other people within hearing distance. The insult had been so vicious, and so uncalled for, that Tony felt there was no way to respond to him—verbally, that is.

But Tony has his own method—a nonverbal one—of dealing with this kind of thing. He waited a little while, then located the drunkest person at the party and took him aside for a few minutes. Not too long after that, there was an unfortunate "accident." Tony had paid the drunk five dollars to spill his drink on the man who had insulted him!

Putting a contract out on someone at a party may not be your style, and I am not condoning it. Certainly most insults are much less aggressive than the one Tony experienced. Most of the time you will just want to take the high road and walk away. However, you may have witnesses to the insult and feel the need to respond to keep the respect of the others around you. In this case, the best way to handle someone who has insulted you is to hit him immediately with a snappy comeback like the ones that follow. As you can see, they range from the corny (which can diffuse a tense situation) to the biting (which may be more satisfying to use). *Warning:* Make sure you have actually been insulted before using any of these lines. They are only for self-defense!

- "I'd hate to have your nerve in a tooth."

- "I think the rudeness police have a warrant out for your arrest."

- "Are you this mean to everybody, or am I just lucky?"

- "What charm school did you graduate from?"

- "My mother always said I shouldn't talk to strangers; now I know why."

○ *"Are you a good witch or a bad witch?"*

○ *"I think your mind has been poisoned. Perhaps it will spread to the rest of your body."*

All-Purpose Lines for Treating Panic

Having supplied detailed advice and instructions for every conceivable set of circumstances, I do recognize that there are times when many people simply feel general mingler's panic. You may be terrified because you've suddenly realized you don't understand what is being said to you; you may be confused or feel you have lost your place in a conversation (and can't remember the Dot-Dot-Dot Plot). You may suspect you've been insulted but just aren't sure. You may have a blind urge to run and don't even know why. Well, don't worry. There are a few simple lines that—while they're not very sophisticated—can save you when you are suffering from a panic attack. When you feel that freezing terror hit you, try to gauge the atmosphere you're in and pick the most appropriate of these lines:

○ *"You know, I love your voice."*

○ *"I'm dizzy. Is it hot in here?"*

○ *"What you say makes sense."*

○ *"Hmm. Life is so interesting."*

Cutting Your Losses (or, When to Just Give Up and Go Home)

The best poker players know when to fold. No matter how much skill you have or how much desire to play the game, sometimes it's simply not in the cards for you to mingle. Occasionally you can tell after only

ten minutes that you should never have come to that particular function on that particular night. If you stay, you are going to end up having a bad time and—what's worse—it's going to be harmful to your
self-image, because you are apt to mingle badly. So if you're too tired,
too sick, or too distracted to put the right amount of energy into the
experience of being at a party, realize this quickly and act on it. In
other words, cut your losses and go home.

Make very certain, however, that you are not throwing in the towel
simply because you are *afraid* to mingle. Many people pose as intro-
verts who can't be bothered with socializing when really it's because
they're all frozen up with terror inside. Learning to recognize your
own minglephobia is an important step in learning and mastering the
art of mingling.

If you do decide to call it quits on a particularly ill-fated evening,
don't let the experience prevent you from welcoming future mingling
opportunities. Everybody skips a party now and then. But always remember that every new gathering—like every human being—is totally unique and unpredictable. You don't want to risk missing what
may turn out to be the best time you ever had.

7 Mingling in the Twenty-first Century

Let me make one thing perfectly clear: *IMing is not mingling*. E-mailing is not mingling; text messaging is not mingling; chatting in Internet chat rooms is not mingling; talking on cell phones is not mingling; photoblogging is not mingling. Mingling has not changed since the beginning of time: it's real people gathered in a real room together, conversing face-to-face.

Cyberspace and other information technology practically define the new century; we have more methods of communicating than we ever imagined possible. The illusion that this makes us more connected comes in part from the knowledge that we can set up a webcam in our living rooms and seconds later millions of strangers can see us. We can trade messages instantly with people on the other side of the world. We can find answers to questions at the touch of a button. We have interactive computers, interactive television, interactive voice mail, interactive everything—but are we really interacting with each other? In the future we will probably be able to dial up a hologram date, talk to Europe on our wristwatch TV phones, or use the USB chips in our heads to communicate telepathically. It still won't be "mingling" unless our corporal bodies are in the same time/space continuum.

All this new technology affords us tools for reaching out to one another and at the same time gives us the false sense that we are really communing. When I tell people I write books about mingling they invariably ask me, "Did you do one on mingling in cyberspace?" And I respond, "Remember cocktail parties? That's what I write about." But people don't have cocktail parties anymore; they are too busy on their computers!

Not too many years ago parents believed that they could teach their babies a foreign language simply by playing audiotapes next to their cribs. What the parents found out was that the babies would tune the tapes out, just as they would background noise. The only way this osmosis method of teaching would work was if there were an actual person presenting it to them. The moral of the story? Nothing will ever replace live people. But between channel hopping, surfing the Web, shopping on Ebay, and downloading Internet porn, people's aptitude and desire for mixing with real-live people are lessening. Most people are doing six things at the same time and have trouble concentrating on any one of them. They feel increasingly isolated, yet they won't make the commitment to talk to a real person they might find right in front of their faces. I used to love talking to cabdrivers in New York City; I would learn something about their lives, and vice versa. Now every one of them is on his cell phone.

I am not a Luddite, I promise. I am, in fact, addicted to my own cell phone. (For one thing, it helps me get to the party!) And I'll admit that the Internet can be helpful for finding people with whom to mingle and places in which to mingle. People are inventing all types of new and wacky parties: speed-dating parties, eye-gazing parties, naked mixers, and pitch-dark dinner parties. After all, there is a reason "temporary" is part of "contemporary." Mingling may be the same as it ever was, but the accoutrements—the menus and venues of minglers—are always changing. What people chat about at parties is, of course, different today than it was fifty years ago. For one thing, politics is now a dangerous curve lurking in the path of every topic.

And in the wonderful new world of mingling, you have to be equally prepared to talk about nanites as you are about nannies.

NAVIGATING CURRENT EVENTS

Keeping up with the issues, trends, and news of the world is what makes us good citizens and better humans. It's ultimately essential to our global health. Ignorance is not bliss; ignorance is ignorance. When the proverbial aliens finally arrive and ask us, "What the hell are you people doing with this planet?" it will be no defense to say, "Gee, we weren't really paying attention."

It's both easier and harder to keep up with today's news. With one thousand TV channels to watch, the Internet to surf, and millions of CDs and DVDs to play, we are bombarded with such an endless stream of stimulation and information that it's hard to process it all. Besides newspapers, we have dozens of cable news channels, thousands of news Web sites, hundreds of news radio stations—an inundation of sound bites and video images. We are exposed constantly, even while waiting in line at the bank, riding an elevator, or visiting a public restroom. Yet most of us know less about what's going on than we should, partially because of the "one-story" nature of the major media and partially because in our quantity-not-quality way of operating, we are used to skating on the surface of things. Or maybe you don't know what's going on because you've spent all your leisure moments for four days watching the complete first season of *Sex and the City* you just got from Netflix.

In any case, it's always advantageous in any interpersonal exchange to understand something about what is being discussed. You don't want to find yourself standing at a party, a drink in your hand, and a dumb look on your face, cut off from the flow because you aren't up on current events. Unlike many conversational experts, however, I do not advise you to tear desperately through newspapers and magazines right before the party. My feeling is that either you're tuned into the world around you or you're not. No amount of last-minute cramming is going to make you a better-informed person. Besides, all of us are bound to have periods of time when we are oblivious—whether it's because we have been swamped at work or have been mired in a personal crisis.

You need to forgive yourself for not knowing everything. However, there are some situations in which you may feel truly mortified that you don't know or can't remember what people are talking about— like a major scandal involving one of your own state senators or a just-signed peace treaty between two countries that have been fighting for a long time, if only you could remember where!

Don't worry: There are some relatively simple strategies for dealing with those moments where you are suddenly and horrifyingly aware that you don't know what in God's name people are talking about (and you really should!).

The Zeitgeist Heist

Let's say you are standing in a group of several people. Suddenly you realize the conversation has taken a turn and everyone is talking about a major mud slide. And not just any mud slide, but one that happened just two days ago and has been in all the papers and on all the news stations. It's a major event that you have somehow missed. People in the group are turning to you, expecting you to put your two cents in.

Your best bet in this situation is something I call the Zeitgeist Heist. The first step in the Zeitgeist Heist is listening—not just to the facts but to the *feeling* behind the facts. You need to determine the issue or the theme of the conversation. Let's say in the case of the major mud slide that after a minute of listening to the discussion you are able to ascertain that the theme of conversation is *not* the tragedy itself but the fact that an increasing number of people are building houses where they

shouldn't be allowed to build them. (Good: You've identified the Zeitgeist.) Then at a suitable moment you offer a remark regarding a resi-
dential area *you* know about in Delaware where they are building homes
too close to the ocean and so have to keep bringing in more sand dunes
lest the houses get washed away. In all likelihood, the conversation will
grow from there and your ignorance will never be spotlighted.

The Zeitgeist Heist differs from a traditional subject change technique because it is a way of joining in rather than distracting from—
it's about keeping in sync with the *spirit* of the discussion. You are
contributing, because your comment corresponds to the sensibility of
the conversation. Is the issue the scandal of the thing? The tragedy?
The politics of it? Are people more focused on how the media is re-
porting the story? It can be just as important to be in step with the
essence of the discourse as it is to be up on the specific details of an
event.

Please note: Make sure you have correctly comprehended the
conversation before you jump in. I once had an extremely pleasant
fifteen-minute discussion with a friend about croquet—until we both
realized that *he* had been talking about cocaine! (He said rich people
love to do it; I said it makes people mean; he said it's hard to find a
place to do it. . . . Every comment we made was appropriate for each
of the two very different subjects! Until finally he said, "I've seen a
drawing of the molecule," and I knew something was wrong.)

Pleading Guilty

Of course, the other thing you can do (and what I often do) is throw
yourself on the mercy of the court. Covering up takes too much energy, and confessing your ignorance is the quickest way to become better informed on the subject at hand. After the initial embarrassment,
you may be able to catch up to everyone. They may even admire your
courage in admitting you don't know what's going on.

Say, "I didn't have a chance to read the paper or see the news today. . . . Where was the mud slide?" Or: "Oh! I think I heard a piece of that on the news today—but I didn't get any details." Or even: "Everything in Washington depresses me so much I confess I haven't been reading the paper at all and don't have any idea about that." (*Note:* Apathy being a national epidemic, this excuse is risky; some people may have little sympathy. And the embarrassment involved in admitting you can't remember who your own congressperson is may be too much to endure.)

Proving Your Mettle

OK, so you don't know about the worst disaster to happen in weeks. That's pretty bad. However, you can partially recover your equilibrium, perhaps your dignity, by proving you have some knowledge on *another* news story. This way people will think you may have a weird lapse in your cultural awareness, but you are not an idiot.

After the initial fervor of the mud-slide conversation dies down (and after having admitted you knew nothing about it) you say something like: "That's what happens when you don't read the paper for a few days. But say, did you happen to read the amazing story in the *Times* a few weeks ago?" And then you proceed with what must be a very interesting news story—one that you *do* know.

I had a story I used to use in this situation. It was a story I had read in *The New York Times Magazine* about a biotech company in Montreal that had bred 150 goats with a spider gene. The resulting goats were able to produce a unique protein in their milk, and that milk was then used to make fibers for bulletproof vests. I had been so fascinated by the story that I remembered small details—for instance, that the resulting goats were only one-seventy-thousandth-part spider and that even that small amount of arachnid genetic material was enough to put spiderweb capability in the goats' milk (!)

and that the fiber would have a tensile strength of three hundred thousand pounds per square inch.

If you can lead the conversation around to a story like this one—a story that is not only unusual and fascinating but about which you can remember intricate details, it works really well as an embarrassment salve. Your story has to be fairly recent in order for you to toss it into the conversation, and it's important for this face-saving routine that you know the story, whatever it is, in depth. This shows you are not a lightweight and that—in spite of your being oblivious to the aforementioned mud slide—you do know how to read a newspaper. Also, it introduces a new topic to the group.

Warning: High-Voltage Area! Talking Politics

We've heard the old adage a million times: Never talk politics or religion at a social gathering. Our mothers drummed it into our heads (at least mine did), as did their mothers with them. The assumption is that these are two areas people feel very strongly about and which aren't subject to normal rules of logic and pleasant debate. People tend to disagree—especially when it comes to politics—in a more disagreeable manner than they do at any other time. Most people will admit that while a difference of opinion can be stimulating, yelling and name-calling can really wreck a party.

Also, when you are at a large party, you are supposed to be *mingling,* ideally. That is, having conversations that are brief and plentiful. Once you start talking about next year's election, you're liable to forget all about circulating. But by far the most serious danger is the emotional one; many people, when talking politics, reach their boiling point quickly and find themselves saying things they hadn't planned on saying. When two or more guests start arguing, it can cause a kind of air bubble at the party; people nearby will turn and stare or, worse, join in—then your discussion can interfere in everyone's mingling pleasure (like the time my friend's uncle Henry ruined the Christmas party when he got into a political argument and threw the turkey at his brother, yelling that birdbrains should stick together).

The dangers of talking politics are more prevalent than ever before, because issues in our country have become more and more polarized. Increasingly, there seems to be no middle ground. At my family gatherings we used to have interesting heated discussions about politics; we now never talk about it. Everyone knows it's like lighting a fuse in a house full of explosives. The problem is that now we don't fight, but our conversation tends to be boring.

In Victorian days, every gentleman or gentlewoman learned the two safe topics for polite conversation: the weather and *your* health. Now even these once-benign areas are doorways to talking politics: The hot topic of global warming is a hop, skip, and a jump from an innocent comment about how warm the weather has been recently, and a courteous inquiry about someone's health can easily become a debate about the health-care system. An innocent remark about someone's new fur hat or the Columbus Day parade can slide you right into politics before you can say "cheese and crackers."

The fact is that there is hardly any way to really avoid talking politics. So although mingling is for the most part supposed to be a lighthearted affair, mingling in the twenty-first century is bound to be a little less superficial. After all, what would be the point of mingling if all we ever talked about was the color of the drapes? Our lives are too closely connected with politics to avoid the subject entirely. How can intelligent people gathered together for conversation totally avoid touching on foreign policy, congressional activities, oil policies, or homeland security issues? The 2000s *are* politics. So I believe it's about time we rewrote the time-honored golden rule to read: It's fine to talk politics and religion, just *don't argue violently about politics and religion*.

Talking politics has its minefields, but it can be worth it for the interesting conversations you can end up having. However, you do have to know how to negotiate your way through the dangers (I am not going to differentiate between religion and politics because they have become so closely intertwined):

1. **Know your own boiling point.** This is extremely important. You have to be certain that you can recognize that moment when you are about to go over the edge into anger—a very hard thing to pinpoint when you are in the middle of talking about nuclear proliferation—and stop. It's a bit like trying to stop drinking before you get drunk; when the moment comes, you can't relate to why you were determined to stop in the first place. If you don't think you can do this (or if all your friends tell you can't), then go back to the original rule. Don't talk politics.

2. **Test for friend, foe, or fanatic.** Even if you are capable in most circumstances of keeping your head, you have to be very careful with whom you talk politics. While it takes two to argue, I don't know many people who can stay serene when confronted with a fanatic. These days a lot of people will fall into that category. To help you spot one before it's too late, you should develop some test questions to administer to the person. These are designed to let you know if (a) you are talking to someone who believes more or less what you do, which is usually fun, if not a learning experience, (b) you are talking to someone from the other camp but who seems open-minded, or (c) you are talking to someone who is going to become belligerent. You can analyze his or her response to decide if you think the water is safe. Keep a close watch on facial expression and body language; it can tell you more than verbal response. The following test lines are just suggestions; this testing device, more than any other, requires your own personal touch. *Warning:* These tests are never foolproof. People's belief systems are not always as straightforward as you expect:

○ *"What newspaper do you like to read?"*

○ *"What news channel do you like to watch?"*

○ *"I just bumped into someone who looked exactly like [name of current political figure]."*

○ *"I heard they don't serve this dish in the White House."*

○ *"Last night I had a dream about the president!"*

○ *"I wonder why blue is for Democrats and red is for Republicans."*

○ *"Did you happen to catch the recent White House press conference?*

3. **Be a diplomat.** Imagine that you're a foreign diplomat at an international cocktail party. Try to remain impersonal and cool, with observations such as, "Our economy certainly isn't doing too well now," rather than, "Are you trying to tell me that we're not in desperate trouble economically?!" A good rule of thumb is to avoid asking *questions* about politics (unless they are truly informational, such as "Have you read about the bill Congress just passed?") and not let your voice get any louder or faster than it would be if you were talking about dessert.

4. **Learn how to defuse and escape.** The minute you feel yourself losing control or when you realize your partner in the political dispute has lost it, *defuse and/or escape*. This is not beginner stuff. Once again, you have to *want* to stop. (Breathing deeply may help, as will moving to another place in the room or getting somebody else to join both of you. Remember: *Change equals movement; movement equals change.*) Here are some examples of lines you can use either to defuse the situation and go on talking about something else (not that likely if one of you is in emotional overdrive) or to defuse and escape:

○ *"Well, I don't know about that, but there's one thing I do know about: I'm hungry! Will you excuse me?"*

○ *"Well, I guess we can't solve the world's problems in one night."*

○ *"Listen to us arguing! No wonder my mother always told me never to talk politics at a party! Do you want to get a drink?"*

○ (Jokingly) *"Well, I guess we'd better either talk about something else or step outside!"*

The most important thing to remember when you decide to talk politics is your mingling objective (the one that should always override all others): You are there to have a good time, not to solve the world's problems or change anybody's mind (which you can't do anyway). So, shake hands and come out *not* fighting.

AHOY POLLOI:
MINGLING IN PUBLIC PLACES

Ignoring the early training of childhood, I make a habit of talking to strangers whenever I am out in public. Not all mingling is done at parties. You never know what interesting people you may meet if you just take the initiative.

Years ago I attended a Pavarotti concert in Central Park. I was supposed to meet up with some friends who had gotten there several hours in advance. Unfortunately, I had misjudged how large the crowd would be; by the time I got there it was wall-to-wall blankets, with hardly any space to squeeze through. As I tried to move forward through the sea of people, I was met with annoyed comments at every turn. I realized that everyone thought I was just trying to get a space closer to the stage—in other words, line jump. What with the thickness of the crowd and the mood of the audience, I knew I was going to have a hard time getting to my friends. (This was before cell phones—today I could have at least obtained some coordinates.)

Luckily, I had with me two delicious homemade apple pies. I began by stopping and sharing a small piece of my pie with a couple of women closest to me. I chatted with them awhile, then moved on to another group of people; I soon gave someone else a taste of pie. People were jammed so close together that the word spread that someone was giving away pie. I used my piece-of-pie offering—along with some serious mingling—to keep moving forward. I was able to explain, along the way, that I had friends up ahead who were saving a place for me. I met numerous people that day and had a grand time. I finally did manage to reach my friends, although all I had left of the pie was the empty boxes!

Next time you're stuck in a crowd, waiting in line, or just hanging out at a café, hit the schmooze button. Even if you happen to be pie-less.

Mingling Outdoors or in a Crowd

Every so often we find ourselves by ourselves at outdoor concerts, train stations, bus stations, amusement parks, beaches, parades, fireworks displays, shopping malls, or Herald Square at Christmastime. You have to be there anyway, so why not mingle a little? Mingling in these situations is very much like mingling in a crowded party (see "The Sardine Can," p. 134), except, of course, since you are out in public, you will find that people will feel more vulnerable and therefore will be a little more cautious. Her are some tips:

○ *Ask for help.* Ask people for directions, for advice, or for information. Most people are happy to be of service, and you could end up having a nice time in addition to getting the information you need. Not too long ago I was trying to get from Manhattan's Upper West Side to Brooklyn on the subway. Due to track work, there were confusing "service changes" (transit speak for "it's just impossible to get there right now"). I was totally flummoxed; and of course, I was late. After a few frantic moments, I spotted a friendly-looking young couple to ask for advice. It turned out that they were on their way to the same neighborhood! I traveled with them all the way (we had to transfer several times). We had a wonderful talk; I interviewed them for this book, and we exchanged numbers. The subway trip was like a fun party, and the experience left me with a definite postmingle glow. It wouldn't have happened if I hadn't decided to ask strangers for help.

○ *Commiserate.* Complain about the train that's broken down, about how long the band is taking to start up, about how many jellyfish are in the water, or about how noisy or hot it is. Misery loves company.

○ *Form a tribe.* If you manage to find a few like-minded people nearby, form a little group and hang out for the duration. With the right attitude you can make a party anywhere.

Lines in Line

It seems as though we are spending more and more time waiting in long lines: store checkout lines, ticket lines, restaurant lines, and the most daunting and torturous line of all: the line for the ladies' room. Long lines can be tiring, frustrating, and boring—a real waste of time. But they don't have to be. Because almost every one of those tedious experiences can be turned into a mingling event!

Think about it. You've got all those people, standing together not talking to one another, for the most part; and they already have one thing in common: whatever you are standing in line for. That's more of a beginning than you have at many parties, where sometimes the only thing you have in common is the host. Many people immediately whip out their cell phones on line to pass the time; why not look around you instead and see what happens?

I would not say that mingling while on line is easy; there are many obstacles, not least being the very fact of the line itself. You are basically trying to mingle without the use of your legs. Many techniques— escape, for example—are drastically different when you are in a line. You have to overcome people's natural suspicion of you (a lot of people are uncomfortable if a stranger starts talking to them in a public place), plus you must be prepared for your conversation to be overheard by the entire line. When you mingle in a line, you are usually conversing directly with only one or two people, but you are almost *performing* for a large group—who, because they are not at an official mingling function, feel no compunction about standing around eavesdropping.

However, mingling in lines can be very rewarding, and because you will probably never see any of these people again (famous last words!), it's relatively risk-free. Here are some specific rules and sample lines for the various on-line mingles (an * signifies that the line is generic; it can be used for any of the following line situations):

○ *Checkout lines.* People in checkout lines can be tough customers, depending on what they are buying. Many people put on their personal armor when they are about to purchase something. If what they've got in their basket or cart looks a bit strange or personal to you, don't mention it. You're going to have to be very nonthreatening and incredibly nice when you deliver your opening line. Be sure to smile wider and more often than you might normally.

In most checkout lines (like those in grocery stores) you are strictly limited to the person in front of you and the person behind you. If all the lines are long and you have a choice, why not choose the line that has the most interesting-looking people in it, rather than the one that is going to get you out five minutes faster?

Here are some possible lines for when you are checking out:

"Oh, I love that stuff."

"It looks like you're having a party."

"Are you going to carry all that yourself?"

"Is this the express line?"

*"Have you been waiting long?"**

*"Do you ever wonder how much of our lives is spent in lines?"**

○ **Ticket, restaurant, and movie lines.** Waiting in line for an event is a good place to mingle, as you are waiting in line for something pleasurable. People are usually in an excited, anticipatory mood. Or everyone is feeling impatient. A word of caution here: Most people don't like to hear other people complain about having to wait in line ("How much longer is it going to be? Why don't they let us in!") unless the comment is witty or funny or meant to inspire a sense of camaraderie. Always remember, unless you are dealing with the Truly Arrogant, conversation while mingling should be good-natured. Sample lines:

"Have you heard good things about [name of the movie or restaurant]?"

"Have you guys been here before?"

"I always feel funny, standing in these lines by myself!"

"This better be worth it!"

○ **Ladies' room lines.** These are by far the easiest lines in which to mingle. Women standing in the seemingly endless, inevitable line for the ladies' room bond together with only the slightest encouragement, because all of them are equally exasperated at having to stand in line to go to the bathroom and probably miss the beginning of the second act as they always do. I've met some great people in ladies' room lines, but I find the conversation doesn't vary much. In fact, what I do in ladies' room lines is sometimes more like organizing a revolt than mingling. Lines:

"When I become president, I'm going to totally revamp women's rooms throughout the nation."

"Ten more minutes of this and I'm hitting the men's room."

"They want a definition of Purgatory? This is it."

"If men all had to stand in line to go to the bathroom for just one month it would change the world forever."

Please note: Bank lines and post office lines are not good places for talking to strangers; people are usually too anxious about taking care of business.

Elevator Mingling

I have always found it disturbing that people seem to have trouble talking to each other in elevators. We enter this little room, stand close together, stare tensely at the display panel, and breathe a sigh of relief when we get out. Most people tell me there's a good reason for this behavior: Our personal space is so infringed upon that our barriers are up. That's reasonable; after all, it is a very small space to be standing in. But if you think about it, you are standing no closer to people in elevators than you are at a crowded party. The difference is that you are in a tiny room that moves and does not seem altogether safe. Everyone is mildly anxious. It's a transitional experience, and people just want it to be over. Well—why not mingle away that anxiety?

It's a new century, folks! We have to get over our elevator stiffness and take advantage of these golden opportunities to interact. I believe people are secretly desperate to learn how to elevate their elevator time. So if you're ready for new frontiers, here are the rules:

1. **Say hello.** It's important to greet everyone in the elevator as you enter and also to greet people who get on after you. You'll be surprised at how people will warm up to this. Always accompany your salutation with a smile. (Your smile will have to be a bit more impersonal than one you would use at a party, especially if you are the only other person in the car. You don't want to scare anybody.)

2. **Include the entire elevator in your conversation.** If you are getting into the elevator with someone else or you discover someone you know in the elevator, don't ignore the others present. This will be a challenge for most, as people have always found it acceptable to have a conversation with another person almost as if there weren't four other people standing right next to them! I have always thought this behavior bizarre and alienating, and it's time it stopped. Your attitude should be that you and your friend have just joined a new group of people at a party. Turn toward the people already in the elevator (only slightly; most people who haven't caught on yet to the proper social behavior in elevators will all be facing front, so your turn must be gentle). Make brief eye contact with people—as you greet them and then once in a while during conversation—but only for a microsecond. The smaller and more crowded the elevator, the less eye contact you should make.

3. **Never make jokes about the elevator breaking down.** It's helpful to use humor to dispel the tension that exists in any

elevator situation, and it is tempting to joke about cable breaks and electronic failures, but *don't do it*. It may get a laugh out of most people, but it could push the claustrophobic right over the edge.

4. **Talk about:** the sluggishness of the elevator, the decor inside, or the doorman of the building, if there is one. Also, if you are in an apartment building, you can comment on someone's mail (not personal mail, but magazines you happen to spot). For example, I once took a long elevator ride with someone who was carrying a copy of a computer magazine; we had a very nice chat about the best kind of scanner to buy. Elevator rides are, for the most part, short, so don't forget to begin your mingling when you are waiting for the elevator (heaven knows, that could increase your mingling time to fifteen minutes). Here are some lines to help you get started:

"Excuse me, but do you work [live] in this building? I haven't seen you before."

"Is there a thirteenth floor in this building? . . . No? Is that a way of dating the building?"

"We've all got to stop meeting like this."

"Do you lose your stomach [Do your ears pop] in elevators or is it just me?"

As usual, these lines are not to everyone's taste. You may want to start up a conversation by simply saying, "Nice weather we are having." The point is, whether you are stuck in an elavator with two other people or you are in Coney Island with two thousand, do not miss the chance to connect with the people around you. Work your mingling magic, and you never know who you may meet.

MINGLING FOR LOVE

There is really no secret at all to mingling for love. It requires the same skills and attitude as any other kind of socializing—except that you might want sexier lines and lower lighting.

One day I was talking to my single friend Sue. She had been to a party the night before.

"So did you mingle?" (I always ask this of my friends; I can't help it. I've got mingling on the brain.)

"There were no single men there," answered Sue.

"That's too bad. But did you mingle?"

"There *weren't* any men, I told you!"

"But did you *mingle?*" I persisted. At last she got my meaning.

"Oh well, yes, of course. In fact, I met this really interesting woman in my business . . ."

Mingling is mingling. (And, dot-com connections notwithstanding, sometimes love is what happens to us when we are busy doing something else.) You never know where your "dream" man or woman is going to come from; he or she could end up being the brother or sister of someone you meet at tonight's party. The more connections you make, the better your chances are for finding a mate—and the better it is for your life in general.

Let me put it another way: Imagine that you knew you were going to meet the love of your life two years from now. What would you do in the meantime? What most people would do is just enjoy life to the fullest—pursuing the things you love, meeting people whenever there is an opportunity—and this is what you should do, too.

Nevertheless, it won't hurt to go over a few basics for the single minded.

Venue Tips

Here are a few tips for doing the single-mingle in particular settings:

○ **Bars and restaurants.** I've heard of restaurants where it is completely dark and you can't see the food (where this is done on purpose, I mean); I've been to bars where the music is so loud that flirting is frankly an impossibility without cue cards. If you are looking for sex and think conversation is old-fashioned, then a sensory-deprived atmosphere may be fine. But I believe if you are looking for a relationship, you should make a habit of hanging out at places that have soft-ish lighting and soft-ish music. Otherwise you may miss it when someone is making advances!

A sneaky pickup ruse that works well in restaurants and bars is the Tourist Trap. This daring (and morally questionable) ploy requires a little bit of acting ability but can be fun. In the Tourist Trap, you play the part of someone who is just passing through town, even though you actually live around the corner. Approach your victim with some version of, "Excuse, me, I'm in town just for the weekend, and I was wondering if you guys knew where the best place is around here to get a hamburger [a good vegetarian meal/a great cup of coffee]."

More often than not, this approach will solicit a friendly, "Well, hey, why don't you just join us [me]?" If it doesn't, you can simply say, "Thank you," and try again with someone else. Of course, if he or she *does* ask you to join him or her, you will have to lie about a lot of other things, like where you work and where you are staying and what brings you to this fair city. (You may find it gives you a thrilling sort of feeling.)

One of the nicest things about the Tourist Trap is that it provides you with a built-in excuse to be at a bar or restaurant by yourself if you happen to be a person who feels funny about things like that. Also, if you should realize at the end of the night that you were all wrong about the guy—that he's not your type after all—you don't have to worry about his calling you. You can send him back into the fray with a casual, "look me up if you ever get to Chicago."

○ **Cafés.** Basically we are talking Starbucks. Say what you want about the evils of big chains, these are actually wonderful new mingling venues. You are allowed to sit for as long as you want, and many people go there alone to work or check their e-mail. The tables are so close together that it is usually easy to start up a conversation. Caffeine comments are easy to come up with ("I hope they gave me decaf!"), as are remarks about the weather outside, how long it takes to get a cup of coffee, or the unbelievably loud noise made by the cappuccino machine.

○ **Stores.** Stores are excellent places for talking to strangers. Everyone is looking at the same merchandise—so you already have something in common. You can't always trust the salespeople, so it's quite natural to ask opinions of your fellow shoppers. If you are a woman looking for a man, a computer store is especially fruitful; there you are, amid all that daunting technology and hardware—no wonder you want company and comfort! I once chatted up five or six men at J&R when I was shopping for a new laptop. In a clothing store, you can ask other people's opinion of what you are thinking of buying ("Does this look OK?"). Or there's always the corny: "Pardon me, but I need a man [laugh] . . . I mean, I need a man's *opinion* on this."

Home Depot and other similar megastores are great for pickups; in the vast alienating universe of Costco or IKEA, who wouldn't want to reach out to talk to strangers? Houseware stores are especially good because you can communicate the fact of your singlehood fairly quickly during your conversation about the linoleum tiles.

○ **Museums.** Museums are trickier; while many people there alone would not mind company, there are people who simply want the peace and quiet and solitude of the art. You do, of course, have all the subject matter you need right up there on the walls, but remember, keep your voice low and your cell phone off. Try a line like: "Those aren't really Georgia O'Keeffe's hands in that picture, are they?" Or, "Excuse me, but I find this piece so disturbing; does it affect you the same way?"

Romance Copilots

Looking for romance can be so daunting that many people will take a companion along for moral support. In this case there are two choices: You can go to the party with another person who is looking for love, or you can take a wingman.

Wingmen or wing girls (also known as "pivots") are platonic friends you take along to help you mingle for love. Many men find it is easier to meet a woman when they have another woman at their side. Women also find it easier to meet men when they have another man at *their* side. These allies can provide cover for you, as well as an entrée; they act as buffers, prescreeners, and shills when you are approaching love prospects. If after talking to a prospect for five or ten mintues you decide you aren't interested, your wing can act the part of your mate and give you an easy out. If, however, you *are* atttracted to the prospect, your wing can help you be levelheaded and make sure it's safe and advisable to proceed. Wings can help get information, as well as promote you to the prospect.

The other option is taking a fellow romance seeker along. This can be very comforting; the person is in the same emotional place you are, and it's fun to compare notes. However, be sure you don't end up competing for the same romantic prospect. It's usually not worth ending your friendship over. I know all's fair in love and all that, but if possible you should try not to get in the way of your friend's game. Women deal with this by talking to each other in advance of approaching a man ("I've got dibs on that tall man with the pipe!"); frankly, I've never been able to discover *how* men deal with it. They probably go off in a corner and do paper-scissors-rock.

Love Lines

If you're looking for love, you're going to need some good opening lines especially designed for romance. Some of these are cheesy, but most people *like* cheese:

○ *"I think I know you from a past life."*

○ *"Pardon me, but you have a very strong aura" (make up what colors you see), "which tells me you are sensual, self-confident—and that you desperately want to have a drink with me."*

○ *"Your parents' place or mine?"*

○ *"Do you think the bartender sees me?" (Look helpless and thirsty.)*

○ *"I'm looking for an opening line. Do you have any suggestions?"*

○ *"Excuse me—have you seen a man with a red beard [a woman in a yellow jacket]? I was supposed to meet a friend; I'm afraid he [she] may not be coming." (If he/she likes what he/she sees, he/she is bound to offer to keep you company.)*

○ *"Excuse me, I just wanted to thank you for sending me the drink. . . . You didn't? I'm sorry . . . it must have been some other handsome man [woman]."*

○ *"I came over to ask you what time it was . . . but suddenly, I don't seem to care."*

○ *"Excuse me, you remind me of someone I used to know. Except . . . I think you're even better looking."*

○ *"Please tell me you are single!"*

○ *"If you are married or gay [straight] I swear I'll kill myself."*

○ *(Giving him or her the once-over): "You know, I had just decided to give up on men [women] forever. Now I see I may have to revise that position."*

○ *"I was thinking of asking you for the time, but I'd rather have your phone number."*

○ *"So where've I been all your life, anyway?"*

○ *"I'm breaking my rule about talking to strangers . . . anyway you don't look that strange."*

○ *"I'm not the kind of woman [man] who approaches men [women] I don't know. Well, OK, apparently I am!"*

Always remember: Whether you are mingling at the health club, a self-help workshop, a convention, or a good old-fashioned cocktail party, try not to limit your mingling to potential dates. Your aim should always be to meet as many people as possible. Of course, there's no rule against going back to have a second or third chat with someone you're attracted to. But unless you fall madly in love, circulate. He(she)'ll be more intrigued if you don't cling like a magnet.

If you *should* happen to meet your soul mate and fall in love at first sight, complete with bell ringing and spine shivers, by all means . . . stop mingling for the night.

HOSTING: HOW TO PLEASE YOUR
GUESTS EVERY TIME

The best hostess story I ever heard was about a dinner party during which one of the guests, who had had a little too much to drink, knocked over a full glass of red wine onto the table. The table was covered in a fine white linen tablecloth, and what made the incident even worse was that the employer of both the hostess and the tipsy guest was present. There was a moment of stunned silence and then, quick as a flash, the hostess made a sudden sweeping motion with her hand, knocking over her own glass of wine. "Look how clumsy we all are tonight," she laughed, completely saving the day for the abashed, inebriated guest. Not many hostesses will go quite that far to put their guests at ease. Frequently, it's the hostess herself who is a nervous wreck.

Host Phobia

Right before I'm about to give a party I usually get a terrible sick feeling in my stomach. This sensation of nausea is not caused by sampling too much dip. It is not caused by overexcitement at the prospect of seeing a potential beau or a celebrity guest. No, this is the uneasy feeling that is born solely of the mortifying memories of parties past.

There was that horrible time I messed up the invitations and managed to invite both the current and the ex-boyfriend of my friend Patty. (The ex-boyfriend drank too much gin and wouldn't leave.) Then there was the time I prepared for a cocktail party for fifty and only eleven showed up—that included the neighbor whom I snared at the last minute to try to fill the room. There was the big birthday bash I'd planned weeks in advance, and then at the last minute I was sequestered on a jury, of all things, and had to host the party with two armed guards by my side. Of course I'll never forget the party during which one of my guests (a would-be writer) kept going up to every-one else there and saying, "Do *you* want to be my agent?"

When you decide to host any kind of party you are asking for it. But if you're like me, you'll risk just about anything for the wonder-ful energy you get (not the anxiety, but that *other* feeling) from having a collection of friends gathered together in your home. No matter what else happens, I always try to emulate the famous hostess Elsa Maxwell, who with only three words always made sure her guests felt welcome: "When they arrive," she is quoted as saying, "I murmur, 'At last,' and when they arise to depart I protest, 'already?'"

Above all, enjoy your hosthood. If you are having a good time, chances are your guests will, too.

The Party Coach

We all know people who are fabulous hosts or hostesses: people whose parties you never want to miss and whose houses you never want to leave. What makes them such good hosts? Simple. They do more than open their doors and provide food. They make certain that everyone has a good time.

Any self-respecting host should make sure that his guests are in fact mingling and that no one is left standing morosely off in a corner by him- or herself. The host is, in effect, the mingling coach for the evening and makes it his responsibility to see that people are mixing. Basically, what the host does throughout the entire night is similar to the Human Sacrifice escape technique, except that it is for more al-truistic purposes. He talks to someone for a few minutes, then leads that person over to someone else. A good host doesn't then merely introduce the two people; he offers them something they have in common. In other words, he provides them with their first bit of subject matter, just to get things moving. Then he's off, to do the same thing again for two or three other people he has spotted who aren't talking to each other. Any conversational "singles," be they super shy or overtly obnoxious, must be "married" by the conscientious host—even drunks and bores (the host who's really on the ball will match these kinds up together). Has a minglephobic come to the party? A clever host will offer a minglephobic a job to do; he will get him or her to pass food, hang coats, pour drinks and will make sure the minglephobe is busy with tasks that necessitate interacting with people.

Certainly it's OK for a host to have a little selfish mingle of his own now and then that has nothing to do with helping anybody else have a good time. But the host's personal conversation time per group should be shorter than if he he were a guest, and he must make sure he spends a few moments—no matter how brief—with every single person who sets foot in his home. (Even if it's somebody's cousin who wasn't even invited.) It helps, of course, that a host has no need of exit lines; the mere fact of his being host will allow him to say, "Excuse me," graciously at any time during any conversation. Everyone understands the duties of a host. However, the party giver's real enjoyment should come from watching his own hostly handiwork: the knitting of his friends or colleagues together.

Note: It goes without saying (but I'm saying it anyway) that no host should ever drink too much at his own party. In addition to the many obvious reasons for this, being a host is a major responsibility, like being mother and father to the whole party. You definitely need all your faculties intact.

The Feng Shui of Hosting

Human beings have energy that needs to flow through their bodies properly; a party has energy, too. If you want to create a good and healthy party flow, here are some tips, loosely based on the principles of feng shui:

○ If space will allow it, **place your bar area at one end of the room and your food at the other.** That way people will be forced to move back and forth, and it will do a lot to promote mingling. Or place the bar and the food table in different rooms. The more people have to move around to get what they need, the more kinetic your party will be. (Even better is if you can manage to have maneuvering room around the food table.) If possible, the food and/or bar—as well as most of the places to sit—should be opposite from the doorways.

○ **Create what I like to call a party heart.** If you've invited a lot of people who don't know one another, it is helpful to give your guests a central area around which to gather. Mostly people use the food table for their focal point, but there are other options. I was reminded of this hosting tip at a recent party where the host had cleverly arranged things so that his iPod and computer were accessible to everyone in the kitchen. (His was a large kitchen with a center island.) Everyone clustered around, scrolling through the music selection, talking about their favorite music, picking out tunes. It gave guests a common focal point and a place to keep coming back to. Watching people's faces bathed in the blue light of the computer screen, I felt as if there were a hearth fire by which everyone was warming themselves.

○ **Remember that lighting is very important.** For everyone to feel relaxed and comfortable, you need indirect lighting. If you have overhead light fixtures (that is, light coming directly from the ceiling), try to make sure those are turned off. When my readers protest, "But I want people to really *see* each other," I say to them what Blanche Dubois said in *A Streetcar Named Desire*: "I don't want reality, I want magic!"

8 From Insecurity to Enlightenment: The Tao of Mingling

"The Tao" literally means "The Way." Taoists believe in the following essential paradox: The less worried you are about death, the longer you will live. The harder you try to do something, the less likely you are to do it. When we apply the philosophy of Taoism to the art of mingling, we might say that the more you try to control and think about all your social interactions, the harder they will be. Throughout this book I have offered up many practical techniques, ploys, strategies, tricks, and lines; and now that you've learned them all, I am going to ask you *not to think about them*. That's right: Don't worry about any of them. This may seem like a contradiction to everything I have been telling you. But like a dancer who has learned all the steps or a painter who has mastered the brushstrokes, now you need to let your instincts take over. In spite of my previous detailed instruction, the best thing you can do to dispel your fears is to relax and be in the moment.

The main themes of Taoism are intuition, simplicity, spontaneity, and nature. Primary to the Taoist system is the idea of getting back to your essential state or true nature. So when your mother said, "Just be yourself," it wasn't, after all, such bad advice—as long as she meant not just your true self but your *p'u* self.

P'u, the Chinese term meaning "the uncarved block," signifies simplemindedness or a simple beingness. A person who exemplifies the characteristic of *p'u* is one who looks at the world with wonder, without preconceptions, one who suspends judgment about everything. This person would never be worried that another person wouldn't like him. The idea of *p'u* is that things in their original state of simplicity contain their own natural power and all the cleverness and wit in the world cannot equal the power of someone who is the pure embodiment of his or her inner nature.

Of course, it's one thing to talk about Taoism and it's another to really live it. But let's look at what some Taoist mingling practices might entail.

WU WEI: PREMINGLE MEDITATION

Let's say you've just moved to Boston. You've been invited to a party by the only person you know in your new hometown—a woman who was a college friend of your brother's. You are going to the party in the hopes of getting to know some new people; however, you've never met the hostess before, much less any of the other people who are going to be there. You are therefore very nervous.

The *Wu Wei* meditation serves the same purpose as a survival fantasy, but here you are going to find the strength from within you rather than from the external world. You can do this meditation at home before you go to the party, in the cab en route to the party, in the elevator, or even while walking up the sidewalk to the front door (but not while driving, please!). It doesn't matter whether or not you've ever meditated before. Try to center yourself and focus on your breathing. Get very quiet and still inside. What you want to do is to get in touch with "the Great Nothing" and become an empty vessel.

Now, I'm not telling you to become empty-headed or foolish. The principle of *Wu Wei* in Taoism is that of nonaction or receptivity (otherwise known as "creative quietude" or "the art of letting be"). The goal is to be in a place of complete receptivity when you enter the party. See yourself as a pool that is being drained of its water. That which is empty gets filled up, so if you are "empty," things—in this case people—will flow to you. This doesn't mean when you get to the party you'll stand motionless and stare with your mouth hanging open. *Wu Wei* does not mean inertia or laziness. It just means you are going to be entirely *present*. It is a sharpening of the mind, an undertaking to perceive the Tao within all things. *Wu Wei* is not inactivity but a *readiness* for action. Don't try to remember any lines or techniques; just know they will all be there when you need them. Just be.

This isn't easy. It takes courage to trust in truly emptying your mind—it goes against what we have been taught about how to use our intellect. By doing this mediation you should be able to at least partially stop your normal preparty internal dialogue: *Now, what was that person's name who is giving the party? . . . Is my tie on right? . . . I wonder if there will be a lot of people. . . . What am I going to say when I arrive? . . . I wonder if they'll have any gin.*

THE YIN/YANG OF CIRCULATING

The yin/yang doctrine is based on the concept that everything in the universe is in the process of becoming its opposite, that there are continuous transformations within the Tao. Life is always turning into death. Wet things are becoming dry; strong things are becoming weak. Remembering this will help you to stay fluid as you mingle, to accept the fact that everything is always moving and changing. In other words you will be better at going with the flow.

Yang is usually seen as light, heat, male, sun, while yin connotes dark, cool, earth, female, moon. But I like to think of it this way: Yang is hello and yin is good-bye. With every hello you experience, there will be a good-bye. With every good-bye, a new hello.

If you fully grasp this cosmic truth about mingling, you will understand that all conversations are temporary. Your hello and good-bye already exist together, like yin and yang. Everything occurs in a cyclical motion; everything is continuous. (And no, I don't mean that the party will never end. This party will end, be it fun or tedious. And there will always be another one later on.) If everything is in the process of becoming its opposite, that means faux pas will soon be triumphs, awkward silences will become bon mots, minglephobia will become confidence, strangers will become friends.

THE ART OF YIELDING: USING THE PRINCIPLES OF TAI CHI (WITH APOLOGIES TO TAI CHI EXPERTS)

I must apologize in advance to dedicated tai chi students who might be reading this, because what I am about to say is an oversimplification. Tai chi is a discipline that is based on going slowly, carefully, gradually, but for the purpose of this mingling technique I have had to condense many of its precepts.

Tai chi is a spiritual practice and martial art that uses the idea of softness, of being relaxed. One of the things my tai chi teacher used to tell the class was that we needed to "walk like a cat." In tai chi you strive for a cat's alertness and a cat's softness. You can spend weeks or years just learning to have your weight centered over the correct part of the feet. Interestingly enough (and though it is probably an etymological coincidence), *ming* means "the name" in Chinese; *ling* means "catlike alertness." It was this definition that first made me ponder the relationship between mingling and tai chi.

Much of learning to mingle well has to do with overcoming fear; similarly, the basis of tai chi chuan is to let go of tension in the body. Not only does relaxing release the tension, but it is through relaxing that great strength and mastery come. Hardness and resistance are the only real obstacles to success. The point is, whether you have just made a bad faux pas or someone has been rude to you or has just made an inappropriate pass, you will not be as negatively affected—or negatively affected at all—if you can employ this important yielding principle. When someone pushes, don't push back; be soft, yield, sink down into your center, and *stay relaxed*. Go with the flow.

Let's say your Boston hostess turns out to be a less than enlightened person. When you get to the party she takes your coat, stares at you, and—in front of several other guests—says, "Boy, I can't believe you are so much shorter than your brother!" (In fact, your brother is six-two and you are only five-four.) Are you thrown off your game? You are not, because, having practiced being fluid and yielding, you bend like a tree in the wind. You smile and say, "Actually, it's my brother who is tall."

In tai chi you also learn to "stick" to the other person, to follow his or her lead. You play with your opponent's energy. (In this vein, another, more playful response to the "short" comment might be a laughing, "And I can't believe *you* are so direct!") Think of everyone you meet at the party as your teacher; jam with them; riff with them; dance with them. See how your music goes together. Feel where they are. But always stay centered in yourself.

HOW TO FEEL HAPPY WHEN YOU ARE LEFT ALONE

Lao-tzu, the founder of Taoism, said, "Silence is a source of great strength." Taoism tells us to focus on the world around us in order to understand the inner harmonies of the universe. The Tao surrounds everyone, and we must listen to find enlightenment.

There you are, at the party of your brother's friend in Boston. Your hostess has pointed you toward the buffet; however, you see that the buffet is crowded and you don't feel like eating anything right away. You are standing alone in a sea of talking people. What should you do?

Nothing. You are fine. Everything is perfect. For the momemt, absorb the energy of the party. If you don't know what to say, say nothing. If you don't know where to go, go nowhere. Taoists are in harmony with the way things really are because of being still and listening. Become one with your surroundings. Soon enough someone will be attracted to your energy and approach. Be prepared to let him or her in, to welcome the chi (the life energy) of the other person. But for right now, do not be afraid of *not* being in a conversation.

When we listen to music there is silence between the notes; it's a welcome silence because we know there is more music coming soon. We anticipate it with joy. The reason it is OK to be standing alone right now is that you know it's by choice and it's temporary. In a sense, not talking to someone when you are at a party makes you appreciate it all the more when you *do* become engaged in conversation. Being content whether you are not talking or talking is how you become one with the party.

When you are really in the zone, when you feel so connected to the party that you get an actual buzzing feeling from it, you have attained what I call the Tingle Mingle. That's when you really get what the art of mingling is all about. Mingling can be a tool to understanding the

Tao. (The Tao is the way to mingling, and mingling is the way to the Tao.) All through this book I have been preaching to you about having a good time. I have tried to reinforce the idea that enjoyment is your only real goal. But actually there's a higher truth than that. Ultimately, mingling well with others is a way of getting in touch with all that is vibrant and wonderful about life.

So mingle on!

Index

ABC of sample lines for continuing the conversation, 36–43
accessories and jewelry, techniques involving, 104–105
advanced mingling techniques, 81–115
  with body language, 99–103
  Bowing, 102–103
  Butterfly Flit (experts only), 90–91
  Case of Mistaken Identity, 91–92
  Fumbling In, 92–94
  gadgets and other paraphernalia, use of, 105–107
  gimmicks for the confident mingler, 91–99
  Hors D'oeuvre Maneuver, 107–108
  the Interruption Eruption (experts only), 94–95
  jewelry and accessories, use of, 104–105
  Mysterious Mingle, 99–100
  Piggybacking, 89–90
  Playful Plagiarist, 85–87
  Pole-Vaulter, 84–85
  with props, 104–10
  Quick-Change Artist, 81–84
  Quotation Device, 95–97

  team mingling, see team mingling
  Toasts, Making the Most of, 98–99
  Touchy-Feeling Mingle, 100–101
  Trivial Pursuits, 87–88
  working the bar or food area, 108–10
Ah, Yes Bow, 102
appearance, choosing to speak with a person similar in, 9–10
Arrogant, mingling with the, 139–41

bar area
  feng shui of hosting, 176
  working the, 108–10
bars, single-mingle in, 168–69
body language
  advanced mingling techniques involving, 99–103
  examining people's, 10
boredom
  career talk, 33
  as reason for moving on, 63
Bowing, 102–103
Buddy System fantasy, 4–5
Buffet Bye-Bye and Other Handy Excuses, 74–75, 142
Butterfly Flit (experts only), 90–91

cafés, single-mingle in, 169
career talk
    boring, 33
    at business functions, 35
    depressing, 34
    opening lines to avoid, 24–25
    repulsive, 33–34
    semiqueries, 35
cell phones, 149
    etiquette, 75–76
    moving on, technique for, 76
Change equals movement; movement
    equals change, 66–67, 69
Changing of the Guard (Substitution
    Illusion), 68–69
changing the subject
    the Pole-Vaulter, 84–85
    the Quick-Change Artist, 81–84
checkout lines, mingling in, 162–63
clichés, using, 52
computer stores, single-mingle in, 169
continuing the conversation, *see*
        conversation, tools and rules for
        continuing the
    conversation, tools and rules for
        continuing the, 29–59
    ABC of sample lines, 36–43
    career talk, *see* career talk
    clichés, using, 52
    Dot-Dot-Dot Plot, 54–56
    the Echo Chamber, 56–57
    eye contact, 53–54
    Funny Thing About Humor, 57–58
    Helpless Hannah Play, 49–51
    Interview technique, 45–47
    name-tag tricks, 43–45
    Playing a Game, 47–48
    recovering from a flubbed opening,
        30–32
    Room with a View, 51–52
Counterfeit Search, 77–78

crowded room, handling the, 134–35
    current events, navigating, 151–59
    pleading guilty, 153–54
    politics and religion, 155–59
    proving your mettle, 154–55
    Zeitgeist Heist, 152–53
Curtain Bow, 103
cutting your loses (or, when to just
        give up and go home), 146–47

daring opening lines, 27
depressing career talk, 34
Dodgeball: the Preemptive Strike, 78
Dot-Dot-Dot Plot, 54–56
dressing wrong, options when, 119–21
drunks
    hosting and drinking, 175
    mingling with, 137–39
dysnomnesia, 122

Echo Chamber, 56–57
elevator mingling, 164–66
e-mailing, 149
emergency escape lines, 79
emergency situations, handling, *see*
        unusual situations, handling
empty party, handling an, 135–37
entrance, making a successful, 13–27
    the Fade-in, 18–19
    fibbing, philosophy of, 15–17
    Flattery Entrée, 19–23
    handshakes, 13–14, 18
    Honest Approach, 17–18
    opening lines for every mood, 24–27
    smiling, 14–15
    Sophistication Test, 23–24
Escape by Mutual Consent, 73
escaping, *see* moving on (escaping)
etiquette of moving on, 65–67
    five rules of survival, 66–67
    knowing where you're headed, 65

exiting, *see* moving on (escaping)
eye contact, 53–54

Fade-in, the, 18–19
Fade-out, the, 68
Fake It Till You Make It, 1–2
faux pas, dealing with the, 118–33
    blaming someone else, 129
    completely ignoring it, 130–31
    dressing wrong, 119–21
    the Faux Pas-cifist, 131–33
    introductions, flubbing, 121–24
    pretending your kidding, 130
    pretending your misunderstood,
        128–29
    recovery lines, all-purpose, 127–28
    storytelling as healing technique,
        124–27
feng shui of hosting, 175–76
fibbing, 15–17, 117
    exit behavior, 66
first clique, choosing the, 7–11
    body language check, 10
    judging a book by its cover, 9–10
    practicing your mingle on the
        socially challenged, 8–9
    safety of numbers, 10–11
flattery
    for the hostess at an empty party,
        137
    Truly Arrogant and, 140
Flattery Entrée, 19–23
food area
    feng shui of hosting, 176
    working the, 108–10
free association, 83–84
Fumbling In, 92–94
funny, trying to be, 57–58

gadgets and other paraphernalia,
    techniques involving, 105–107

Game Playing, 47–48, 136–37
Grateful Bow, 102

hand kissing and other unwelcome
    physicalities, 143–44
handshakes, 13–14, 18
Helpless Hannah Play, 49–51
    handling drunks with, 138–39
Hi Bow, 102
Honest Approach, 17–18
    in Reverse, 67
honesty, *see* fibbing
Hors D'oeuvre Maneuver, 107–108
hosting, 173–76
    feng shui of, 175–76
    host phobia, 173–74
    the Party Coach, 174–75
Human Sacrifice, 71–72, 142–43
Humble Bow, 103
humor
    cautions about, 57–58
    defensive techniques for handling
        jokers, 59
    faux pas, to deal with, 120

insults, handling, 144–46
Internet, socializing on the, 149, 150
Interruption Eruption (experts only),
    94–95
Interview technique, 45–47
introductions
    confessing, then dwelling on it,
        123–24
    flubbing, 121–24
    made with something besides
        names, 124
Invisible Man fantasy, 4

jewelry and accessories, techniques
    involving, 104–105
jokes, telling, 58

ladies' room lines, mingling in,
    163–64
Lao-tzu, 182
laughter, 58
lighting at a party, 176
lines, mingling in, 161–64
love, mingling for, 167–72
    love lines, 171–72
    romance copilots, 170–71
    venue tips, 168–70
lying, *see* fibbing

Maxwell, Elsa, 174
mingling, definition of, 62, 149
Mistaken Identity, Case of, 91–92
Moats, Alice-Leone, 137
movie lines, mingling in, 163
moving on (escaping), 61–79
    boredom and other discomforts, 63
    Buffet Bye-Bye and Other Handy
        Excuses, 74–75, 142
    Celling Out, 75–76
    Changing of the Guard, 68–69
    Counterfeit Search, 77–78
    defusing and/or escaping from a
        political discussion, 158–59
    emergency escape lines, 79
    Escape by Mutual Consent, 73
    etiquette of, 65–67
    the Fade-out, 68
    five laws of survival, 66–67
    Honest Approach in Reverse, 67
    the Human Sacrifice, 71–72,
        142–43
    knowing where you're headed, 65
    optimum mingling time, 64
    in a packed room, 135
    the Personal Manager, 73
    Preemptive Strike: Dodgeball, 78
    saving face, 63
    Shake and Break, 71

    Sit-Down Mingle and, 141–43
    the Smooth Escape, 69–70
    team mingling reconnaissance and
        rescue, 114–15
    the Telephone Line, 75
    twelve exit maneuvers, 67–78
    Vanishing Group, 63–64
    when to move, 63–64
museums, single-mingle in, 170
Mutual Consent, Escape by, 73
Mysterious Mingle, 99–100

names, forgetting, see introductions
Naked Room fantasy, 3–4
name-tag tricks, 43–45
No Nice Girls Swears (Moats), 137

off-color remarks, 58
opening lines, 24–27
    to avoid, 24–25
    delivery of, 25, 27
    level one: the risk-free line, 26
    level three: the daring line, 27
    level two: the playful line, 26
    practicing, 25–26
    recovering from flubbed, 30–32
outdoors or in a crowd, mingling,
    160–61

packed room, handling the, 134–35
panic, all-purpose lines for treating,
    146
partner, mingling with a, *see* Buddy
    System fantasy; team mingling
Party Coach, 174–75
party heart, host's creation of the, 176
Personal Manager, 73
physicalities, hand kissing and other,
    143–44
Piggybacking, 89–90
pivots, 170–71

playful opening lines, 26
Playful Plagiarist, 85–87
Playing a Game, 47–48, 136–37
pleading guilty to lack of knowledge
     of current events, 153–54
Pole-Vaulter, 84–85
politics, talking, 155–59
practicing opening lines, 25–26
Preemptive Strike: Dodgeball, 78
props, techniques employing, 104–10
     gadgets and other paraphernalia,
          105–107
     Hors D'oeuvre Maneuver, 107–108
     jewelry and accessories, 104–105
     working the bar or food area,
          108–10
Pros and Icons fantasy, 5–7
proving your mettle (knowledge of
     current events), 154–55
public places, mingling in, 159–66
     in elevators, 164–66
     in line, 161–64
     outdoors or in a crowd, 160–61
Punctuation Mark (bow), 103
punsters, 58

Quick-Change Artist, 81–84
Quotation Device, 95–97

relaxed, staying, 180–81
religion, talking about, 155–59
restaurants
     lines in, mingling in, 163
     single-mingle in, 168–69
risk-free opening lines, 26
romance, see love, mingling for

safety in numbers, 10–11
Sarcastic Bow, 103
Sardine Can (packed room), 134 35
saving face, moving on and, 63

Serious Terror Inducers, 2–3
Shake and Break, 71
shaking hands, 13–14, 18
shepherding, 113–14
Sit-Down Mingle, 141–43
smiling
     in a packed room, 135
     when entering a conversational
          clique, 14–15
Smooth Escape, 69–70
socially challenged, practicing your
          mingle on, 8–9
solo mingling, 25
Sophistication Test, 23–24
Starbucks, 169
stores, single-mingle in, 169–70
storytelling to mend a mingling faux
          pas, 124–27
Substitution Illusion (Changing of the
          Guard), 68–69
survival fantasies for truly terrified,
          2–7, 140
     Buddy System, 4–5
     Invisible Man, 4
     the Naked Room, 3–4
     Pros and Icons, 5–7

tai chi, art of yielding using principles
          of, 180–81
Tao of mingling, 177–83
     art of yielding, using the principles
          of tai chi, 180–81
     feeling happy when you are left
          alone, 182–83
     themes of Taoism, 177
     Wu Wei premingle meditation,
          178–79
     yin/yang of circulating, 179–80
team mingling, 110–15
     conversational procurement, 111–13
     intraparty play dates, 113

team mingling *(continued)*
  mating call, 115
  preparty strategy sessions, 111
  reconnaissance and rescue, 114–15
  shepherding, 113–14
teasing the Truly Arrogant, 140
Telephone Line, 75
text messaging, 149
Thin Room (empty party), 135–37
ticket lines, mingling in, 163
time period, optimum mingling, 64
Tingle Mingle, 182
Toasts, Making the Most of, 98–99
Touché (bow), 102
Touchy-Feeling Mingle, 100–101
tough rooms, negotiating, 133–41
  drunks, mingling with, 137–39
  Sardine Can, 134–35
  Thin Room, 135–37
  Truly Arrogant, mingling with the,
    139–41
Tourist Trap, 168–69
Trivial Pursuits, 87–88
Truly Arrogant, mingling with the,
  139–41
twenty-first century, mingling in the,
  149–76
  current events, *see* current events,
    navigating
  hosting, *see* hosting
  for love, *see* love, mingling for
  in public places, *see* public places,
    mingling in
  what it is not, 149–50

unusual situations, handling, 117–47
  cutting your loses (or, when to just
    give up and go home), 146–47
  faux pas, *see* faux pas, dealing with
    the
  hand kissing and other unwelcome
    physicalities, 143–44
  insults, handling, 144–46
  panic, all-purpose lines for treating,
    146
  the Sit-Down Mingle, 141–43
  tough rooms, *see* tough rooms,
    negotiating

Vanishing Group, 63–64

wall-to-wall people, mingling in a
  room of, 134–35
white lies, *see* fibbing
wingmen or winggirls, 170–71
Wu Wei premingle meditation, 178–79

yin/yang of circulating, 179–80

Zeitgeist Heist, 152–53